"I believe God is saying to me, 'I am handing you back your life for a demonstration period at the very end, so that a viewer looking on may see if there is anything in it.'"

World-renowned author-evangelist E. Stanley Jones suffered a paralyzing stroke. For five hours he lay totally helpless. Physically, Dr. Jones was a broken man.

Saying "yes" to life, he learned to walk and talk again to the amazement of his doctors. He even preached with the characteristic zeal of his entire ministry. *The Divine Yes* was completed, and Dr. Jones returned to his beloved India where he died peacefully 14 months later.

During his richly active life, Dr. Jones had written 28 books, two of which had become million-copy bestsellers.

The Divine Yes

E. Stanley Jones

**with the help of his daughter
Eunice Jones Mathews**

To Earl —
With gratitude
for devoted service
to the church —
Jack Trull
Christmas - 1977

festival books

**ABINGDON
NASHVILLE**

THE DIVINE YES

A FESTIVAL BOOK
Published by Pillar Books for Abingdon Press

Festival Books edition published May 1976

Scripture quotations unless otherwise noted are from the Revised Standard Version of the Bible, copyrighted 1946, 1952, and 1971 by the Division of Christian Education, National Council of Churches, and are used by permission.

Scripture quotations noted Moffatt are from *The Bible: A New Translation*, by James Moffatt; copyright 1935 by Harper & Row.

Scripture quotations noted Phillips are from *The New Testament in Modern English*, copyright 1958 by J. B. Phillips.

Scripture quotations noted NEB are from the New English Bible, copyright © the Delegates of the Oxford University Press and the Syndics of the Cambridge University Press, 1961, 1970. Reprinted by permission.

Quotation on p. 107 is from *The Terrible Meek* by Charles Rann Kennedy. Copyright 1912, 1933 by Charles Rann Kennedy. Copyright 1939 (in renewal) by Charles Rann Kennedy. Copyright 1961 (in renewal) by Harold J. Gorst. Used by permission of the Owners and Samuel French, Inc.

ISBN: 0-687-10989-2

Printed in the United States of America

CONTENTS

INTRODUCTION

Upon hearing the news of my father's stroke I flew
directly to Oklahoma City. When I reached his bedside and he recognized me, he indicated he wanted to
say something important. In his feeble, almost inaudi-
ble voice he said, "Daughter, I cannot die now. I have
to live to complete another book—The Divine Yes!"
He hoped fervently that this would be possible. Here
is presented the fruit of his faith for he did, indeed,
live long enough to complete his final message.

It was only a short time before his death that he
brought to a conclusion all that he could do with the
manuscript. It must be understood that he was confronted with almost insurmountable handicaps during
his last fourteen months: sight, hearing, speech, use of
one arm, locomotion—all were impaired. At first he at-

7

tempted to write the book in his customary fashion by longhand, for he could use his right hand. But since he could not see clearly enough to guide his hand, the words ran together and were indecipherable.

Finally, it was decided that he should dictate the book into a cassette tape recorder. This proved successful and was at the same time a kind of self-therapy. The tape was played back to him, and he was able thereby not only to correct the copy in some measure, but, more important, to effect rather remarkable improvement in his quality of speech. However, since he was interrupted frequently by the hospital regimen, continuity of thought was difficult to achieve.

After months in hospitals in and around Boston, our family, at his request, helped him return to India. He dictated other portions of the manuscript there. Various people helped in the transcription. A number of drafts were read back to him for correction, and attempts were made to correlate the material in a more orderly way.

Upon his death the manuscript was brought back to me. Clearly what he wanted to say essentially had been written. Nevertheless, it lacked the organization, coherence, and order which he could not achieve with his handicaps. Interspersed in the margins from time to time were little notes addressed to me, "This does not belong here, but you'll know what to do with it." Through the years I have typed most of his manuscripts, and both my husband and I are familiar with his style and content. But this was a different and more difficult assignment. Much reordering and even deciphering were required.

At first it seemed impossible to see how the book

could ever be prepared for publication. We spent considerable time on it during the summer of 1973, but without success. The manuscript simply would not "hang together." It was with some reluctance that we went back to it again the following spring, determined that somehow we could rearrange the material so that it would be what he intended, and what it really is: a kind of summing up, a spiritual last will and testament. After great effort it was finally possible to organize the material in the present form. Remarkably, nearly everything he had dictated we found possible to use. Somehow we believe the result would please him. My father most earnestly wished to give one more ringing testimony that "Jesus is Lord."

Grateful thanks must be expressed to many people:

To Mrs. Mary Webster, longtime friend and evangelist colleague of my father, who painstakingly transcribed an early draft from the cassette tapes when his speech was almost unintelligible;

To the members of the Sat Tal Ashram who cared for him so devotedly, in body, mind, and spirit;

To the doctors and nurses of Clara Swain Hospital in Bareilly, India, who gave him their best in loving care and medical science;

To Tunnie and Eloise Martin, missionaries in Bareilly, and their household staff, who gave so unstintingly of their time and love in his last sickness;

To his many friends in India, in the United States, and around the world who not only upheld him constantly in their prayers during this final illness and throughout his years of activity in God's work, but supported his work materially as well;

But particularly to my husband, James K. Mathews,

without whose constructive suggestions and creative ideas the publishing of this book would never have been possible. Few people are as well acquainted with my father's thought and expression as he is. At a time when we were in complete despair as to how to handle a manuscript which had no real breaks or proper sequence of thought, my husband one morning was truly inspired as to the format which could be used. His help has been invaluable.

As a prelude to the material he dictated, we have included a sermon, "The Divine Yes," which he preached many times, especially in his later years. This version is pieced together from several tapes of the sermon and written material we have found. Essentially the book is organized around a number of questions which call for an affirmative answer. These are authentic queries. They emerge from real life and from the depths of the human search. These are not all of the problems which plague human existence and trouble the human spirit today, but they are among the important ones. As is often said, "Christ is the answer, but what is the question?" He is the affirmative to such inquiries as these arising from inner deeps. Jesus Christ is the Divine Yes!

My feeling and hope is that this book will prove of particular help to many kinds of people. Among these are the seriously or chronically ill, the discouraged, those who feel themselves badly used of life, or those whose lives seem to have caved in on them. But others, too, should find divine aid and inspiration here. I refer to those earnest seekers after light and truth, old and young alike, who search for solutions to the profound, age-old questions which always address those who take the gift of life seriously and responsibly. They need not despair, for the Divine Yes has at long last been sounded.

Eunice Jones Mathews
Lent, 1974

Washington, D.C.

THE SERMON:
THE DIVINE YES

"The divine 'yes' has at last sounded in him, for in him is the 'yes' that affirms all the promises of God."

II Corinthians 1:19-20 (Moffatt)

Jesus is the Yes—the divine Yes. A great many people today would like to choose Christianity, but they think it is a No to living. "You cannot do this." "You cannot do that." "You cannot do the other"—if you are a Christian. This is in fact a denial of the will to live. It is the will to surrender and die.

So listen to my text: "The divine 'yes' has at last sounded in him, for in him is the 'yes' that affirms all the promises of God." That will be the title of my next book. This verse says it is a divine Yes. And it says it has been at last sounded. Because before Jesus life was a No. The ancients did not know how to say Yes.

The greatest No was Buddha. He pondered deep and long on the problem of suffering. He came to the conclusion that existence and suffering were one. The

13

only way to get out of suffering was to get out of existence. The only way to get out of existence was to get out of desire. Cut the root of desire—even for life—then we go out into that actionless, passionless state of Nirvana, the state literally of the snuffed-out candle.

Once I asked a Buddhist monk in Ceylon, "Is there any existence in Nirvana?" He said, "How can there be? There is no suffering; hence, there is no existence." Nirvana is giving a vast No to life. Buddha would get rid of our life problems by getting rid of life itself—get rid of your headaches by getting rid of your heads. This note of tragic negativism also runs through almost all Japanese drama. The atmosphere of Japan and Eastern religions is No, No, No!

Then the Vedantic Hindu wants to get beyond the personal to the impersonal, Brahma. So he sits and meditates and says, **"Ah hum Brahm, Ah hum Brahm, Ah hum Brahm"** ("I am Brahm"). But the Brahm is the impersonal. It is not a Him; it's an It. The Vendantic philosophy says concerning Brahma that the highest one can say is **Neti. Neti.** "Not that. Not that."

Then to both the Buddhists and Vedantists the world is **Maya,** an illusion. It is not real. Therefore you cannot change the unreality. It is play that in Hinduism is called **lila,** the play of God. What you think is reality is not reality. It is like a magician creating an unreal, illusory world around you.

The mood of the present day is cynicism. Many people are soured on life. They are cynical and negative. This age has three sneers for everything and three cheers for nothing. It has a code of "I don't believe in this;" "I don't believe in that;" "I don't believe in the other." They are trying to live by a No. And it is turn-

14

ing out badly and sadly, for you can't live by a No. You have to live by a Yes.

Bertrand Russell said that life is a bottle of very nasty wine that leaves a bad taste in your mouth. A great actor was dying and said, "Let down the curtain, the farce is over. There is no reality in life; it is a farce." Sartre, the French existentialist, said, "Hell is other people." How can you have a society if you believe other people are hell?

Furthermore, modern materialism comes to a similarly negative conclusion. A very able man who was a chemist and the head of the chemistry department of a great university said to me that man is nothing but combustion, chemical combustion. He flares up for a few years and then dies down to an ash. I said to Dr. George Carver, the great Negro saint and scientist: "You are a chemist. What would you say in reply to this man—that we are nothing but chemical combustion?" He said, "The poor man, the poor man." That is all he would say. It was a very adequate reply, because if you have a small view of life, a poor philosophy, you are going to be a poor man. If you believe that the end of life is only an ash, then you are going to live life as an ash. A Nothing.

Now is Jesus a Yes or a No? If he is No we cannot take him, because we can't live by negation. We have to live by affirmation, for we are affirmative beings. We can't live by No and cynicism.

After these ages of No, No, No comes this statement from Paul, perhaps one of the greatest that he ever wrote: in him, Jesus Christ, at last, at long last, of No, No, No, has come an affirmation—the divine Yes has sounded! Over against these human No's a divine Yes

15

has sounded, for in him all the promises of God find their Yes. He is the divine Yes—not a human guess, but a divine Yes! Does he affirm all the promises of God? Yes!

1. Now let us look at some of the promises of God. I was in Russia, and I went through an antireligious museum. When I got through I turned to the Russian guide and said, "Do you think this is an adequate answer to religion? I think it is a terrific No against the organized system of religion built up around Christ, but you haven't come to the real thing yet—Christ and his Kingdom." She said, "No, I don't believe it is adequate as an answer, but our scientists are putting up another museum. In this they are tracing the genesis of religion from magic and superstition. That would be an adequate answer."

I said, "I am not so certain because you would conclude too much. You are going to get rid of religion because of its lowly origin? But what about other things? Where did the modern surgeon come from? He came out of a medicine man dancing around a fire, muttering incantations. Are you going to get rid of the modern surgeon because he came out of that? Where did the modern astronomer come from? He came out of the astrologer, a pseudoscientist trying to read your destinies in the stars."

Of all the foolish things that the newspapers print today, the most absurd is the horoscope business. Five million people in America try to decide their destiny according to the position of the stars—as if lumps of matter floating in space could decide the destiny of a spiritual being made in the image of God and with the power of choice! When you haven't got enough nerve to make your own choices, you turn to the stars and planets and let them make them for you. This is always a sign of decay.

Are you going to get rid of modern astronomy because it came out of that? No. That is a pseudoscience, not a genuine science. When you get rid of religion because it comes out of magical and lower forms, you have to get rid of other orders of society for which lowly origins could be found.

But I don't believe that religion has come out of magic and superstition. It takes magical and superstitious forms again and again, but I believe the genesis of religion is in an urge for life. Tagore says that everything lifts up strong hands after perfection. I conclude that the religious urge is that life urge turned qualitative.

We want to live not only more fully but better; the moment we say better we have standards, and the moment we have standards we have religion. As long as people want to live fully and better we will be religious. In fact, we are incurably religious. Jesus is the divine Yes to that. He has at last sounded to that urge after life. He said, "I am come that they might have life, and that they might have it more abundantly" (John 10:10 KJV).

2. A second thing I notice about Jesus is that he is the Yes to God. Many have had a question mark as to whether or not there is a God. The Buddhists say, "We don't mind using the idea of God, or rather believing in the idea of God, but we don't use it because if we do use it, we may taint it." They believe that God is so holy and infinitely above us that mankind may taint the concept. Now Jesus, instead of tainting the idea of

God by using it, simply and quietly said, "He that hath seen me has seen the Father." Then I say, "Is God like Christ? If so he is a good God and trustable." I couldn't make God any better than what I see in the face of Jesus.

I was in a Hindu temple and there were frescoes around the walls, rather crude. I remarked to the pujari, the man in charge of worship: "Do these frescoes help you in your worship?" He replied, "You have to be very strong to come into this temple to worship. Otherwise you might go out and do what the gods do as depicted on these walls." "Oh," I said. "Man is going to rise higher than his gods. Show me your gods and I will show you your man." Inwardly I said to myself, "Isn't it wonderful that I can look into the face of Jesus Christ and know what my heavenly father is like!"

A little boy was in the States while his father and mother were across the seas as missionaries. Christmas Day came and the principal of the school said to himself, "That boy will be homesick for his parents." So he went to see the little boy and said to him, "What would you like most of all on this Christmas morning?" The little boy thought a moment and pointing to a picture of his father on his dresser said, "I would like most of all that my father would step out of that frame and come and be with me." That is the homesick cry of humanity: "I wish my heavenly father would step out of the frame of the universe and come down and be with me." That has happened! God has stepped out of the frame of the universe, and we have seen him in the face of Jesus Christ. He is God with us. For Jesus Christ is our heavenly Father, personalized—with us.

He is the Yes to that cry of humanity for some power over us.

3. The third Yes is a Yes that human nature can be changed. This, too, is a promise of God. Some people in the East and West think human nature never changes. It is fixed and unchangeable, and you are destined to be what you are. Jesus gives a New Birth in this life. The first birth brought us into the natural universe, and the second birth brings us into the Kingdom of God. This is a change so radical that it is called New Birth.

Jesus said this to a man rather up in years: "Except a man be born again, he cannot see the kingdom of God" (John 3:3 KJV). Nicodemus looked into his eyes and said, "How can a man be born when he is old? Can he enter a second time into his mother's womb and be born?" (John 3:4, KJV). Jesus' answer: No, it isn't that. But you can undergo a new birth in this life. It is birth from above, through the Spirit.

Many believe in rebirth; that is, reincarnation, the notion that you come back birth after birth. The Hindus say one must go through eighty-four million rebirths before you can find God and then be released from the cycle of continuous rebirths. To have to come back again and again eighty-four million times before you are free from this samsara, as they call it, is a somber prospect! It is absurd to believe one must be punished in this birth for misdeeds done in the last birth according to the law of Karma. This belief has placed a paralyzing hand on India as well as the Buddhist countries where this concept is held.

But Jesus said Yes to a new birth. He said you can be born again in this birth. All you have had in a natu-

ral birth is through your parents. Now one may be
born from above.

You don't need to be the kind of person you are.
You can be born anew and this new birth extends to
the conscious and subconscious mind. You can start
anew. The accumulated guilt of the past is removed—
forgiven. You can be released by a new birth. "Therefore if any man be in Christ, he is a new creature: old
things are passed away; behold, all things are become
new" (II Cor. 5:17 KJV).

Jesus is that Yes that you can be different and need
not be the same. But can human nature be changed? It
is more changeable than anything on earth. It is the
nature of human nature to change. The new birth can
turn you from hate to love, from defeat to victory, and
make you a different person. I don't care what you
have been or what you are. Jesus is the Yes to a new
birth.

4.   Furthermore, he is the Yes to the fullness of the
Holy Spirit. We want not only to be born again but to
be able to meet anything that can happen with our
new resources that are full and adequate. These resources give us power to meet everything. This new
power is from the Holy Spirit.

When the Apostles first went into the upper room
after the Resurrection they were timid believers. They
were behind closed doors and full of fear. Even
though Jesus was risen and they had heard the news,
they were caught in elemental fears. Then something
happened: we call it Pentecost. They hadn't won a
person during the three years they were with Jesus,
but in three hours after Pentecost they won three
thousand. Something had happened. The Holy Spirit

had moved into their subconscious mind and cleansed them. Peter before Pentecost kept saying, "They-I." "They might deny you, but not I." He lived in a "They-I" relationship. But when the Holy Spirit came upon Peter he said "we"—"We cannot help but speak the things we have seen and heard." Power had come in—the power of the Holy Spirit. Peter telling what happened said, "This Jesus God raised up, and of that we all are witnesses. Being therefore exalted at the right hand of God, and having received from the Father the promise of the Holy Spirit, he has poured out this which you see and hear" (Acts 2:32-33).

So Jesus is the Yes that God can and does rule in the inmost recesses of our hearts. He is in the subconscious mind which we can't control. There he can cleanse us and make us adequate. So he is the Yes to the fullness of the Holy Spirit. He is the Yes to the upper room. The door is open—through him. And if you take the Holy Spirit, it will make you a Christlike person.

At last, then, at long last the Divine Yes has sounded through him. Jesus is the Yes to all of God's promises: that there is a God, a Father lying behind this universe caring for all creation; that this Father is manifested in the face of Jesus Christ, for ours is a Christlike God; that humankind can be different, and life can be utterly changed; that our emptiness can become fullness as every recess of our inner and outer lives is invaded and empowered by the Holy Spirit. To all these promises Jesus Christ is the Divine Yes, and we belong to him.

If you belong to Jesus, you belong to the Kingdom that cannot be shaken through death or old age. Christianity means to say Yes to his Yes. Surrender to his will and you will be saying Yes to his Yes. The whole universe is behind it. You will walk the earth a conqueror, afraid of nothing.

TO PREACH A SERMON
OR TO BE ONE?

During the years it has been my practice to read
from the Bible daily. It has been more than reading.
Quite literally, it has been to "read, mark, learn, and
inwardly digest" the subject matter. Among the many
legacies left me by the small, evangelical college
which I attended was the insistence on a life of devotion. There, long ago, the habit of devotion—approxi-
mately two hours a day of Bible study and prayer—
was fixed. To this, maturity and refinement—the habit
of listening to the Inner Voice as well as speaking during prayer—have been added. If I have had a secret
weapon, this has been it.

The margins of one Bible after another have literally been covered by the notes I have been accustomed
to making along the way in my quiet time. These, as

well as notes from my rather wide reading and recollection of the day's experiences taken down each night, have contributed to my sermons and books. There the seed was sown.

I liked the text from II Corinthians 1:19-20 from the first time I read it. Moffatt's translation particularly appealed to me: "The divine 'yes' has at last sounded in him, for in him is the 'yes' that affirms all the promises of God." When that version was first made available to me, nearly fifty years ago, I was struck mightily by this verse, and through the years it has grown on me. Naturally I knew I must preach on this great text.

It was not as if I wrote a sermon on it. It actually seemed to emerge and grow and season with the years. I have preached on that text scores of times and, through interpreters, in a dozen or more languages all around the world. Not always was the sermon the same, for obviously it was tempered according to the particular circumstances of the time and place and the needs of the congregation to which it was preached. I believe it has been an instructive sermon for it leads out of life and again into life. It has been a doctrinal and expository sermon, for it does endeavor to expound not only the word of God, but the Word which is God. For the Gospel is essentially Yes, the Divine Yes. It is, therefore, an evangelistic sermon, used of God's Spirit to open the doors of the Kingdom to many seekers.

During my last evangelistic tour in Japan, during the autumn of 1971, I preached it a number of times. But never did I anticipate that I should have to live the sermon after the manner which for the past year I have been compelled to do. What I have proclaimed by voice, I have now found confirmed by life—life in its extremity. Hence, this book, which is a kind of summing up—a last will and testament, spiritually speaking.

This leads me to say that I didn't choose this last call to write a book on the Divine Yes. It seemed a part of the paralytic stroke which has afflicted me. As I thought about it, I came to the conclusion that it had always been part of my life resources and my life plans to be taking up things that I could not do—and then by God's grace doing them. I never dreamed of a stroke that leaves you helpless as a call to present a Divine Yes, the universal Yes which meets a universal need. But perhaps it is in the fitness of things that it should be so.

It may be that I shall fail. "Well," I said to myself, "the cross was a seeming failure made success." And yet the Cross is the center in the Christian faith. So God chose not to save Jesus from the Cross, but to save others through Jesus by the Cross.

So I said to myself that I could fail. So what? Jesus used failure and made it the greatest success because through that failure, God showed his ultimate power. He overcomes evil with good, and hate by love, and the world by a Cross. The Cross was defeat. You cannot defeat defeat. You cannot break brokenness. Jesus on the Cross showed us God's method of redemption. He overcomes evil with good, hate by love, and the world by a Cross through suffering.

God is stripping me of everything to give me Everything, the last everything with a capital E. As I have often said before, I have never written a book without his seemingly addressing through me some basic and fundamental human need. This one will be in line with that succession because the need of humanity is a Divine Yes. Humanity has sunk deeper and deeper into negativism. It is a cynical age, and there is sin in cynicism because it sins against the nature of reality. I believe the Christian Gospel is in accord with that reality.

Once I listened to an expert on Turkish affairs. He spoke of Asa Jennings, a hunchback and an official of the YMCA who had rescued two hundred thousand Greeks from Smyrna in the debacle following World War I when the Turks had defeated the Greeks and were threatening Smyrna. Jennings asked the Greek government to give him ships to take out their people, but the Greeks were afraid that if they gave the ships, the Turks would capture them. Jennings wired that if they didn't let him have the ships by six o'clock that evening, he would tell the world that the Greeks wouldn't provide ships to carry their own people to safety. They wired back, "Hold off. The cabinet is in session."

Before six o'clock the ships were given to Jennings. The American destroyer nearly burst its boiler getting Jennings over to take charge of these ships. He took the ships and rescued over two hundred thousand Greeks from Smyrna. In doing so, he kept the confidence of the Greeks and Turks alike and was decorated by both governments. The expert on Turkish affairs said, "The greatest asset in Jennings is his colossal ignorance of Turkish affairs. He believes in everybody and everybody responded." Seeing his amazing faith in them, the Turks responded to that faith. Everybody else was inhibited by their knowledge of Turkish af-

26

fairs, but Jennings had no knowledge to inhibit him. He had faith. That is exactly what we have to have if we are going to change the world.

Perhaps I can write this book by faith. If it is now hard for me to preach a sermon; why not be one?

A Sudden Stroke in the Night

A SUDDEN STROKE
IN THE NIGHT

December 7th moved into December 8th, 1971. It was to be for me a strange, contradictory day. Life was suddenly changed and spoke in two directions. I was confronted seemingly with disaster; nevertheless, it gave promise of new possibility. It was more than two directions; it had double meaning.

I had just finished a two-month evangelistic tour in Japan. Of course, I had some questions about the advisability of beginning, at age eighty-seven, such a major undertaking, with that country upset as it was at the time by university students. This was my tenth visit to Japan and perhaps the most important one of all. They called it "The Tenth Evangelistic Tour of Stanley Jones." Could I stand up under it? I had my question marks, but also my faith! It needed to be done. However, this tour was blessed more than I could have imagined or thought possible. We went to forty-five cities, and I spoke one hundred and fifty-four times. Moreover, more than six thousand Japanese signed cards making a decision for Christ. Of these four thousand represented first commitments; two thousand of them were renewals.

The sponsoring committee, which represented the Kyodan and the National Christian Council as well as evangelicals of all kinds and including all races, represented the widest backing of any of my ten Japanese evangelistic efforts. The committee, probably having their question marks, gave me a "trial run" the first day of only six speaking engagements to see how much I could take. When they saw I took those six meetings in my stride, they were sure, and so was I. I stood on top of my world. Japan was a country wide open to evangelistic appeal and I, at nearly eighty-eight years, could take it without exhaustion. On the contrary I faced the challenge with exhilaration. Life was very lovely indeed.

Then in December I returned from Japan, seemingly none the worse for wear. I was holding a United Christian Ashram meeting in Oklahoma City in a Roman Catholic retreat center. One evening we arranged a healing service to be held the next morning in place of the morning devotion. In such healing services we ask three classes to come forward for healing: those who want physical healing, those who desire moral and spiritual healing, and those who seek both. Everything seemed to offer promise as we anticipated this gathering.

That night I woke up and had to go to the

bathroom. As I started back to my bed, I found I was paralyzed. The right side of my body was intact but the left side seemed to be completely numbed. In struggling to get back to my bed, I collapsed in the middle of the floor. I remember my arm came around my aluminum suitcase which has been my "home" for many years of travel. And then I couldn't move one way or the other.

I stayed there for several hours in complete collapse, but somehow the right side of me worked enough so that eventually I was able to get back into my bed. There I was just as helpless as ever one could imagine. From about two o'clock in the morning until seven, I was a completely broken person.

At seven o'clock, there was a knock on my door to get me to come to the healing service, but I couldn't answer it. The door was locked from the inside. Since I was on the first floor and the window was partly open, they climbed in and found me. I was, as I say, a completely helpless person with my left arm and leg useless, the right side of my face numb and sagging, sight and speech badly impaired.

They sent for an ambulance, and I was soon in the hands of physicians and nurses at the Baptist Memorial Hospital. The doctors put me under intensive care and assigned me their best nurses who worked around the clock. I thank God I was in such a hospital and in such competent and loving hands.

Up to that night life seemed rosy. I had been a missionary to India for more than half a century. A lifetime of evangelism had taken me almost everywhere. I had written, without intending to be an author, twenty-eight books, two of which had become best sellers of more than a million copies each.

Only a few months before I had finished writing my twenty-eighth book, entitled **The Unshakable Kingdom and the Unchanging Person.** I had inwardly prayed that I might be given strength enough to complete that book and give in it all I thought was my message to cap all the other things that I had been trying to say for seven decades. That strength had been given. The book was already in the hands of the publishers.

I had been trying for more than two decades to unite the Christian Churches around the world upon the principle of Federal Union—unity in diversity. Thousands of informal voters in hundreds of audiences had thought that it was possible to do so. I still feel strongly that this method, or a similar one, is the answer to our search for the shape of church unity.

Besides my evangelistic efforts and books, perhaps one of my principal contributions has been the founding of Christian Ashrams. From our first Ashram in Sat Tal, in the foothills of the Himalayas in India, the movement has spread throughout the world. I will mention this subject again elsewhere in this book.

I looked forward to a gentle descent into my nineties and perhaps beyond with nothing but gratitude for what God has wrought, for I have watched him do it rather than doing it myself. I had endeavored to be a faithful and humble witness to Christ in every situation. Then suddenly: Bang! I found myself and my future apparently in ruins. My means of locomotion were shattered, and I could not recognize my own voice on a dictaphone. The only hopeful thing said to

31

me was that the brain passages which preside over the intelligence were not affected. Everything else had been changed.

But I said to myself, "Nothing has changed! I'm the same person that I was. By prayer, I am still communicating with the same Person. I belong to the same unshakable Kingdom and the same unchanging Person. Nothing has really changed except my means of communication with the outside world."

The glorious thing was that my faith was not shattered. I was not holding it; it was holding me. I could still put up my three fingers and say, "Jesus is Lord!" Everything was intact. I can honestly say I wasn't asking, "My God, why?" I could and I can face the future with him.

A WITNESS IMPAIRED
OR A WITNESS
EMPOWERED?

The most amazing thing that came out of the shattered remnants of that night was this: I could go on. I could still be a witness. Through this shattered situation, I was to write still another book. The text and the texture were clear and breathtaking.

It was to be on the subject of this passage: "The divine 'yes' has at last sounded in him, for in him is the 'yes' that affirms all the promises of God." The title of the book was to be **The Divine Yes.** Now I must say this Divine Yes through the shattering "No" of a stroke. Now I must apply what I have been preaching through the years: that no matter what happens to us, the final result depends on how we take it. Here I was to be called upon to illustrate and apply the Good News, the Divine Yes, in the face of the bad news life often offers—a No. Can two more contradictory things be wrapped up into one event? Can contribution come out of collapse? In the Christian faith can it still be the Divine Yes, no matter what happens?

I found my numbed body and stunned mind taking fire with the possibility of going out of this life with the Divine Yes on my lips as my last word and message: a Divine "Yes" when life was saying a human "No." That would be a contribution for tomorrow.

But to accept a commission such as the Divine Yes the greatest problem lies in the one who accepts it. He must be convinced that the Divine Yes is not only possible, but will sustain one and supply his or her every need. You can't play verbal tricks on yourself; you must really believe it. This can't be an example of trying harder, of whipping up the will. No matter how honest and dedicated, the human will knows its own weakness and limitations.

I felt that I was not accepting something that was contrary to my basic philosophy of life. I had never been called on to illustrate so drastically what I believed and preached—body, mind, and spirit. Now I was just taking my own medicine. A novelist said that the cross of which she was writing is God taking his own medicine. God isn't a signpost pointing the way. He is the shepherd and says, "Come, follow me." It's the Divine Yes.

The Gospel is rooted in the divine and seen in the divine and offered in the divine. It is not a human philosophy, but a divine revelation. That makes it quite different and quite possible if we know how to take it. The thing that I am accepting is the acceptance of the one who himself accepts me. In other words, Jesus is the divine illustration and not just the divine school-master. His teaching is what he does. When he washed the disciples' feet he said to them: "You call me Teacher and Lord." Then note that he reverses the order: "I . . . am your Lord and Teacher" (John 13:13-14 Moffatt). I tell you this: I am not first of all a teacher; I am the Lord who demands a perfect obedience because I am demonstrating to you that very obedience required. What I am, namely, love, I offer to you in my very self.

Let me repeat what the English novelist said: that Jesus is God taking his own medicine at the cross. What Jesus did is proof of Jesus. He offers God to us. Someone said that what Jesus is saying had to be illustrated. It is the Divine Yes which has sounded, shown by the divine showman.

Now I more really believe in what I am accepting and have been proclaiming, While I accepted it as a gospel to be proclaimed, I was never before called upon to accept it fully as a matter to be shown in one's own life. In other words, I've been saying across the years that in the Cross is the Victory, and now I have to pick up that Cross in a new sense and show that it is the Victory!

As I have said, I may fail, but I would rather fail with Jesus than succeed with anybody else, for to be with Jesus is the Victory. He doesn't defend the Victory; he is the Victory. All I have to do is to be grateful in accepting, all down the line, the Gospel that I've preached. I know that to proclaim it is to live it, and to live it is to receive it.

The essence of the Christian Gospel is grateful receptivity. So I'm not accepting something that will change the basis of my life and make me some other person. I actually believe that the Christian way is the way to live and not merely a way to get to heaven.

This is a point of morality then that doesn't produce self-centered boasting, but boasting in what God does and makes us. This is Victory! "I have overcome the world." I overcome in his overcoming; I am good in his goodness; I am love in his love. When temptation and sin come to me and say, "Take me and let me bully you," I say, "Wait a minute! Let me see the back of your neck." On the back of the neck of all temptation, sin, and evil are the footprints of the Son of God. In other words, I receive his victory; I am strong in his strength; I am alive in his life. I am pure in his purity —if I know how to take it. That opens the gate to everybody, everywhere. What it means is letting his goodness produce goodness in us.

It is possible for anybody who is created in his image to be re-created in that image. It is not only possible, but it is his destiny and man's restlessness until he is re-imaged. The central sickness in humanity is homesickness. My own sickness had to be seen in such broad perspectives. I found that I was not merely a witness impaired, but a witness empowered. Jesus is the Divine Yes to all of God's promises and has he not promised: "You shall receive power"?

QUESTIONS WHICH
DEMAND AN
AFFIRMATIVE ANSWER

Is There a God?

The first and most important question concerning
Jesus as the Divine Yes is the ultimate question of
whether or not there is a God. If there is no God, how
did the universal law and order come into being? By
chance—which has been the usual and customary hypothesis of modern theoretical science? But how can
that happen? Could atoms, floating in space, chance
upon universal law and cosmic order, a law and an
order which reach from the lowest cell to the farthest
star and all things in between? Could that happen by
chance? Then you must spell your Chance with a
capital C and mean by it God.

How could it happen that atoms floating in space
would chance to fall into patterns and systems universally valid? Then that would be a materialistic miracle.

37

When I pick up the newspaper or a book and see that there is intelligence in there, I know that back of that intelligence there is an intelligent mind expressing itself through that intelligence. I pick up the universe in thought and see that this is an intelligent universe. It responds to intelligence, so apparently intelligence has gone into it for intelligence comes out of it, and back of that intelligence is an intelligent mind. Since that intelligence seems to be universally minded, behind it must be a Universal Mind. We call that Universal Mind, God.

If there is no intelligence, where do we who have intelligence come from? Out of a nonintelligent universe? Can nonintelligence produce intelligence? If so, that once again would be a completely materialistic miracle.

You and I have a purpose. Could we get that purpose out of a nonpurposeful universe? Can the nonpurposive produce the purposive? If true, it is a miracle as difficult to believe as the nonintelligent producing the intelligent, for like produces like.

But somebody objects and says, "Couldn't evolution account for the whole thing—resident forces in nature turned toward intelligence? Cannot they produce intelligence by chance?" But when you say that, you have to park your intelligence outside, for you smuggle intelligence into the process and try to say that God isn't necessary. But God could use evolution as a method of creation. He could create all at once, or he could create the creation by a slow process. Which would take more intelligence at a billiard table: to put a ball into the pocket by one swift blow, or strike a ball that strikes a second ball that strikes another ball and so on until the last ball goes into the pocket? The latter would take the most intelligence, foresight, and skill. So God could have created all at once by direct creation, or he could have done it by slow developmental processes, or both. The idea of the many gods is gone and the idea of the one creative God takes its place, because the nature of the universe is a universe not a multiverse. The God we accept is one creative God.

12 The Divine Yes Pyramid PA154-9616

Is there a God? The question receives in Jesus Christ a resounding Yes!

Does God Reveal Himself?

But the next question is, Does God reveal himself? We believe that the author of the universe, the one creative God, is seen in the face of Jesus Christ. The question arises: does God show himself? He is a Universal Spirit and we are bounded by our flesh. How can this one creative God show himself to us who are bounded by the flesh? I can see that there are several ways. He can show himself first through nature, and I come to the conclusion that God is law. He works not by whim, notion, or fancy, but by his law and cosmic order. I am grateful that God does not reveal himself by whim, notion, or fancy for we might have a very chaotic universe. The mind that is behind the universe is a mind that works in an orderly way and according to dependable laws.

The universe is lawful and orderly because God's mind is an orderly mind. It is a dependable universe because God's mind is a dependable mind. I am grateful for this: that God is law. But I am not satisfied, for I am not a subject asking for a law. I am a son asking for a Father. I want to know if my Father works, not only by laws and cosmic systems, but by love. Nature cannot tell me if God works by love. Its voice is equivocal or silent.

Nor can a perfect revelation come through prophet or teacher, for the revelation, in going through them, becomes limited, sometimes distorted, because of the faulty human medium. Nor could the revelation come perfectly through a book, for literature cannot rise higher than life—the life that surrounds the literature puts content into the literature. So the book would be pulled to the level of our highest experience. Then, the only complete way of revelation is through a life—a character which would show us what God's character is like. That character is Christ—the human life of God, that part of God we have been able to see.

The Bible then is not the revelation of God. It is the inspired record of the revelation. Otherwise, the revelation—the word become flesh—would be printer's ink. The revelation is seen in the face of Jesus Christ.

Nor is revelation merely a philosophical system, however subtle. For example, philosophy reached an acme in the Hindu philosophers. They strained their minds to grasp the Infinite and came to the conclusion, the startling conclusion, that all they could say about God is **Neti. Neti.** "Not that. Not that."

One day one of the disciples said to Jesus, "Show us the Father, and we shall be satisfied." Jesus said, "He who has seen me has seen the Father." (John 14:8-9). He didn't say, "Not that. Not that." He said, "Now here, Now here," and he pointed to himself. For Jesus is God's revelation of himself. He couldn't have said anything about himself more wonderful than to say, "Yes, he who has seen me has seen the Father."

"Show me your gods and I'll show you your men." We cannot be at cross purposes with God without being at cross purposes with the universe and ourselves. Therefore, what God is like, we must be like or we are going to get hurt.

The chairman of one of my meetings was Governor "Soapy" Williams. He told this story, and I have never forgotten it. He said his son was carrying a heavy rock across the yard. He called his son and said, "Son, why don't you call upon all your resources?" The son protested, "But Dad, I am!" The father said, "You haven't asked me to help you." The son's resources included the father's resources, but he hadn't laid hold on them.

We have to rediscover the resources of God that make us bring faith out of the faithless and bring belief out of the beliefless and bring love out of the loveless. Somebody defined democracy as that madness which believes about people that which isn't true, namely, that they can govern themselves. Yet without that belief, man would not be able to create the kind of men out of which democracy can be made. Faith creates the thing it believes in. And that is what Jesus is to humanity. Wherever he goes praising God, people and life begin to spring up.

Paul says, "The life I now live in the flesh I live by faith in the Son of God" (Gal. 2:20). So there is a Divine Yes because the possibilities are ripe and life can produce a good life and overcome the cynicism of life. Religion needs this. In The Methodist Church they

41

used to have an "Amen corner." Whenever the preacher said something worthwhile they would say "Amen." It gave an "Amen" atmosphere to the service. Now the Amen corner has disappeared and instead of saying "Amen" people say "Oh yeah?" The atmosphere is no longer creative. It is a damper instead of a doer.

One of the things they said of Jesus was that he was a light, sent to enlighten the Gentiles. Another way of putting it is that he was showing the possibilities to the Gentiles. He came to create faith in God and faith in man and faith in the possibilities of people. So I present Jesus as a faith that is working faith in people and their possibilities. It is a plus and not a minus. You can't live on a minus sign; you can only live on a plus sign.

If God is like Jesus, he is a good God and trustable. If he isn't, then I don't care for him. I turn to Jesus when I imagine the kind of God I would like to see in the universe. I couldn't imagine anything finer or more wonderful than what I see in the face of Jesus Christ. So at long last we see the universe simplified to one word: Jesus! When we do, the universe claps its hands and says, "Of all the revelations, that is the most revealing. Of all the statements, that is the statement that states most. Of all the conclusions that men have come to, that is the most conclusive conclusion." God, in character, is like Jesus, and thus he loves people like Jesus loved people and gave himself for men as Jesus gave himself for men. If that is true, then all other truths fade into insignificance. This is truth become Truth, and love become Love, and life become Life. Hallelujah!

In the Divine Yes about God, Jesus gives us the picture, the presentation of God that should be reasonable to any reasonable person. It is not only reasonable, but the most attractive presentation of God ever made—or that ever could be made—on this planet.

Is There a Corporate Dimension of Revelation?

A third question is significant, especially in our day. If God reveals himself personally through Christ, what of the corporate dimension? What is the collective ideal? How is that revealed? Through the Kingdom of God. The nature of the Kingdom of God is determined by the nature of the social order in which that Kingdom operates. The Kingdom operates silently, but decisively.

The character of God's realm is Jesus. Jesus went out preaching the gospel of the Kingdom of God, and he preached the gospel of himself. He was the Gospel, and the Gospel was the Kingdom. He didn't bring the Gospel; he was the Gospel in his own order and in his own person. Now this is unique, absolutely unique! No other religious teacher ever made himself and the Kingdom of God the same. Why? Because that lays upon him the claim that the Kingdom is as himself, the obligation to be the embodiment of that Kingdom. But who dares to be the embodiment of that Kingdom? He dared for he was the embodiment.

Jesus not only said, "He who has seen me has seen the Father," but implied that he who has seen me has seen the Father's Kingdom—has seen it in me. This is either breathtaking blasphemy or breathtaking revela-

43

tion: that he is the New Order, embodied. So when Jesus proclaimed himself as the New Order, the Kingdom of God and its embodiment, he made his Gospel relevant. Therefore, the most important thing today is to present something that is totally relevant—individually and collectively—and embodied in a person.

I believe that Jesus is a Yes to the Kingdom of God. The Kingdom of God is Christlikeness so universalized we can think of nothing higher and we can be content with nothing less. It makes our faith totally relevant in the total situation at all times. Therefore, you don't have to try to become relevant. You are relevant, as you believe and obey, preach and proclaim the Kingdom of God embodied in Jesus.

Of all the unique elements of the Christian faith presented to the nonChristian world that I have heard, the Kingdom of God is the major uniqueness of that faith. Yet it has seldom been presented head on and adequately. No other faith dare present the Kingdom of God and dare to present the embodiment of that Kingdom. It is too heavy a burden to carry. But Jesus carried it because he was it, and it was no burden. It was just the Gospel.

One time I said to a leading communist in Kerala, South India, "The two things in your communist program—the best things that it offers and that make communism float—both came out of Christianity. The two things are these: (a) distribution made according to each person's need, and (b) contribution from each according to each person's ability. Both are voiced in the Acts of the Apostles." So those two things—distribution according to need, and contribution according to ability—are the two best things in communism and they both came out of the Christian faith.

I said, "You communists took hold of those two things and embodied them in your system and put physical force behind them. But when you put force behind them, you corrupted both of them. Therefore you made, not a new order on earth, but a new warfare on earth. You tried bringing it in by force and corrupted it. You had better come back home." He laughed.

It is, however, no laughing matter. Here is a system, resistant to the Christian faith, that has borrowed from Christianity the two most important and valuable things in it, but corrupted by physical force. So the Kingdom of God is the real issue in the world today—the Kingdom as represented by Jesus and embodied in love. If we don't take it, we will continue to have the mess we have now.

The Kingdom of God is total and its rules demand total obedience. In India years ago a maharajah made a law that every man under him in his kingdom should obey the law of monogamy: one man, one woman. But he himself took a second rani, a queen. The people objected. The maharajah's answer was, "I make laws, but I don't obey them." Democracy came. The people rose up and put him out as ruler on the basis of his hypocrisy.

The Kingdom of God is quite different. God made the laws and Jesus, the Incarnate God, didn't just stand and proclaim those laws, but incarnated them, showed them in action demonstrated them with perfect freedom. Everything that Jesus taught, he embodied. What he demanded, he obeyed. In him the law

45

was life. But, he created human beings with the freedom of choice, risking the possibility of disobedience to the cosmic law on which his Kingdom was based. When we do his will, we do the very thing for which our human nature is made. Is it the natural way to live? True. When you do the will of Jesus, you are blessed by it. When you do something contrary to it, you are poisoned by it.

Moreover, its laws are written on the human frame and even from a physical standpoint are inexorable. For example, a teacher committed adultery with a woman and told me later that he went up the hill trembling from head to foot. Why? No one saw him. No one laid blame on him. The Kingdom of God said, "You are wrong!" His physical frame trembled because of that inner tribunal.

We are seeing around the world in a glare of burning buildings and devastated landscape the handwriting on the wall: "Thou shalt love thy neighbor as thyself." There are two hands, the hand of grace and the hand of judgment. What we will not take from the hand of grace, we will have to take from the hand of judgment. This is the hour of judgment, when every wrong is being exposed and every heart that is trying to uphold that wrong is in trouble with itself and the world. So we are discovering the Kingdom of God everywhere. The handwriting is the same everywhere.

The world demands and is ready for such a dynamic, living Christ and his Kingdom. I was in Peru and they showed me the court where the judges sentenced the unbelievers. At the side of the court on the judges' seat was a wooden statue of Christ. When the judge made the judgment and decree, the head of Jesus would nod in affirmation, making Jesus affirm their judgment. It was a wooden Christ, not a real Christ. It failed for they had nothing but a human institution behind it and that isn't enough.

The Book of Acts ends with these words: "Let it be known to you then that this salvation of God has been sent to the Gentiles; they will listen. And he lived there two whole years at his own expense, and welcomed all who came to him, preaching the kingdom of God and teaching about the Lord Jesus Christ quite openly and unhindered." (Acts 28:28-31). When Paul said, "they will listen," he meant they will listen to a twofold affirmation: the Kingdom of God and the name of the Lord Jesus, a new Order and a new Person, the absolute Order and the absolute Person. It was this twofold emphasis that he was saying they would listen to. And we must listen to it! The individual Christ is wonderful. The individual Kingdom is also wonderful. But when the two come together, the absolute Order and the absolute Person, it is absolutely wonderful—wonder of wonders! God speaks in these two ways in total answer to man's total need. We will listen! People will listen again. They have listened to portions of the Gospels, but now they will listen to the whole.

To the presentation of a personal Christ without a Kingdom-of-God Christ, they have listened, but in a dissatisfied way. They say, "Yes, here is the answer, but why doesn't it answer the total needs of man's total life?" It is because the total Christ and the total Kingdom of God have not been presented. When it is presented in one total package, man will listen because of dire necessity. Nothing else has ever satisfied.

47

So the time is right for people to listen to Jesus, who is the Divine Yes. Were he a human yes, we'd look at him and say, "Yes, you are the best that humanity has produced or will produce, but what is behind you? Are you the Divine Yes? Is God and his Kingdom behind you? If so, we will listen, all ears and with all allegiance." They won't listen to half answers any longer. They will only listen to the total: the absolute Order and the absolute Person, giving one total answer to man's total need. When we present this, they will listen.

So Jesus is the Divine Yes to the necessity for a New Order on earth and for that order being embodied, because he is not a verbal Yes. He is a vital Yes. He is an incarnate Yes.

Is There a Right Way to Live?

For many years I have been emphasizing that there is a redemptive purpose running through nature as well as history. The Ten Commandments are not merely written in the Bible, but in the constitution of reality. They are written in human destiny and physiology. This is to say that the universe is one of moral consequence: you reap what you sow. Another manner of expressing this would be that the Christian way is written into the very structure of the universe. It is likewise written into the structure of human relationships. There is a right way and a wrong way. Furthermore it is written into living tissues—nerves, arteries, organs, cells. If we offend against laws of hygiene or health, the laws are not broken; we are! The same is true of all the laws written into the universe. There is a Way and there is a Not-the-Way. Jesus, the Divine Yes, is the Way. In fact, the Kingdom of God and the Way may be used synonymously. Is there a right way to live? Yes!!

When Jesus says, "I am the way" (John 14:6), he means that he is the Way for God and for man. It is not only the Way to God but the Way of God. Jesus shows us what God is like and what we can be like. The Christian Way is the way of God, the way God chose in coming to us, and we have to learn how to take and not to achieve, how to appropriate an inner receptivity.

A man at eighty-two with a lovely face (and it is an achievement to have a lovely face at eighty-two—you are not responsible for the face you are born with, but you are responsible for the face you die with. Every man is responsible for his own face after forty!) said, "When I put myself and my life in the way of Jesus, I knew it was the Way for I was no longer fighting with myself." He and himself, in the Way of Jesus, were akin and therefore he was at peace with himself.

A friend came down the stairs one morning and said to his guest, "John, I do thank God for you." John thoughtfully replied, "Well, I do thank God for myself." He was no longer at war with John. John was now on the Way, the laws of whose being were his own laws. Therefore, he was a happy, adjusted man.

A woman in Sweden said, "I dislike myself. I even hate myself. But I have to live with myself." Then one morning after making a surrender to Christ she said, "Do you know, I love everybody this morning, including myself. Strangely, I like myself now." She, too, was on the Way. A little girl said, "I like the kind of self I'm becoming, in contact with Jesus." In other words, when you find the Way, you find yourself. It is your native land.

A little boy was found weeping. They asked him what was the matter. He said, "I've been playing hookey all day from school, and I just found out this is Saturday!" So when you play hookey against the Way of the Kingdom you play hookey against yourself. The prodigal son said he had sinned against heaven, the impersonal moral law, and against himself; against the laws of God and against the laws of his own being.

A theologian said, "The Christian Way is sense. If you try any other way, you are not only a fool, but a damned fool. I'm not swearing when I say that. I am telling the truth."

So the whole idea that the Christian Way is the hard way is totally wrong. It is the other way that is the hard way. A man came to Sam Jones, the evangelist, and said, "I only know one verse of Scripture, and I know that one verse is true. It is, 'The way of the transgressor is hard.' I know this is true!"

Yes, the idea that the Christian way is hard is all wrong. His yoke is easy and his burden is light, for his yoke is your yearning and his burden is your blessing. When you find him, you find yourself. The laws of your being are the laws of the Way. The Kingdom of Heaven, the Way, is within you and is the thing for which you were made; and therefore, when you find him, you find yourself. There is more joy to the square inch in being his than there is to the square mile in the outside world of rebellion.

A friend of mine remarked about another: "She looks

as though she had swallowed an electric light bulb— she is so luminous." When doctors asked her, "Are you allergic to anything?" she replied, "Yes, I am allergic to sin." A profound statement and very true.

A surgeon said: "I have discovered the Kingdom of God at the end of my scalpel. It is in the tissues. The right thing morally is always the healthy thing physically." I said to the doctor, "Say that again. You said something profoundly important."

Someone said of the nineteenth century Hindu reformer, Keshab Chandra Sen, "He has a New Testament face." He had, indeed, been profoundly exposed to Jesus Christ and his teachings.

John 8:34 reads in the Revised Standard Version: "Truly, truly, I say to you, every one who commits sin is a slave to sin." This is an important passage for it says that any man that sins is a servant of sin. This brings us to the crux of the question which is of great importance to the Christian faith, Is sin natural or is goodness natural? Are we structurally made for sin or for goodness? This passage tells us that any one who sins is a slave of the sin. He is not fulfilling his own nature, but rebelling against the nature of reality.

The basic Christian doctrine is: God created man in his own image. "In the image of God he created him" (Gen. 1:27). That is man's true nature. But man has corrupted that nature by sinning. Sin is a custom, but the unnatural; it is an intrusion into the laws of nature and is basically unnatural. The Bible says, "The natural man receiveth not the things of the Spirit of God." (I Cor. 2:14 KJV). The word "natural" is wrongly translated. It is **apneuma**: "The **unspiritual** man receiveth not the things of the Spirit of God." (Revised

51

Standard Version). It should be translated unspiritual
man instead of natual man. Basically we are made by
God and for God.

A psychiatrist called up a pastor and said, "Can you
help me? My patients are hanging their faith on me as
though I were God. They call me at two, three, or
four in the morning just to talk to me. I cannot stand
this any longer. It's getting on my nerves." The pastor
suggested he read The Way, one of my books. He read
seven pages and was soundly converted. Before this
happened he was charging people $50 an hour for an
interview. He immediately cut down the charges to $8
an hour and was so excited over living a Christian life
that he did a good deal of free work. Jesus was the
door, which immediately opened.

People are anxious to find the Way to live—a true
and living way. Two Christian workers went out to do
visitation evangelism. They were jittery because one
man on their list was a leading lawyer. They came to
him and asked him to join the church. He asked, "Is
that all you want of me? If so, I have nothing more to
say except no. Many have asked me through the years
to join the church, but I have never done it. If that is all
you want, I have no response." They said, "Well, there
is this other side of surrender to Christ, but frankly we
don't know much about that ourselves. So we have
come on the only level we know, church membership."
The lawyer said, "I read something in the church
paper that said you would have a decision card with
you—a decision to commit my life to Christ. Do you
have one?" They handed him one, and he signed it,
saying, "I've always wanted to do that, but no one has

ever asked me to do it. They have always offered me something different or less."

He asked them where they were going next and if he could go with them. He ended up going through the whole visitation evangelism campaign. Now when people come to him to get a divorce, he gives them a copy of **Abundant Living** to read for a week. If at the end of the week they still want a divorce, he listens to them, but not in the beginning. Here is a man who wanted to be totally confronted by the total gospel for total allegiance, and he represents many. They will listen if there is something big enough to listen to.

When Jesus finished his Sermon on the Mount, in which are the laws of the Way, he said, "Every one . . . who hears these words of mine and does them will be like a wise man" (Matt. 7:24). Not merely a good man, but a wise man. If you are a Christian, a real one, you are a wise man. And if you are not, you are a fool, fooling yourself by sinning against your own being, against your own happiness.

When I came into this Way of the Kingdom, my first feeling was to hug myself that I had sense enough to do it. I still feel that way at the age of eighty-eight and sitting in a rehabilitation hospital recovering from a stroke. My eyesight is cut in half, my speech is barely intelligible. My locomotive powers are almost nil. I am having to learn to walk again like a baby. But am I unhappy? If so, I haven't discovered it. I belong to an unshakable Kingdom and an unchanging Person. My feet are on the Way. Jesus is the Divine Yes when there isn't much yes in my surroundings to rejoice in, except in him. In him is the embodiment of the Kingdom. If it isn't, it just isn't. But I am happy because my happiness isn't based on happenings, but is based on him, the Eternal.

People will listen to a message about the way to live for at least these reasons: (1) We are created by the Creator to live in this Way of the Kingdom and the Person. You cannot live against your destiny written within your nerves and tissues and your general make-up without being dissatisfied and unhappy. We were predestined by our makeup in the image of Jesus. (2) They will listen because nature sides with grace. We are pressed from above by grace and from below by nature. We are squeezed into the Kingdom, as it were. (3) No one will succeed, however implemented, to live against the great design. It is a losing battle. (4) This is an age prone to experiment in living, and all the experimentation will end in taking the best hypothesis. It is the survival of the fittest, and the Christian way is proving to be the best way to survive. (5) There is more joy to the square inch in being a Christian if you are a real one. (6) You cannot live by a No without becoming a No. (7) When you say Yes to Jesus Christ, the universe says Yes to you.

Is there a right way to live? Yes, for Jesus is the Way. As the Divine Yes he reaffirms this fact.

Can Humanity's Deepest Hungers and Thirsts Be Satisfied?

Everywhere and at all times men and women have hungered and thirsted for righteousness, for reality, for life. This is evident today around the world, though it is not always understood to be a religious search. It was true of ancient Athens where its citizens were forever seeking "something new."

When Paul went to Athens, he had the opportunity of his life to present the Gospel in the center of philosophy of that age. He said some good things—God made mankind of one blood and gave them food in their seasons. But when it came to presenting Jesus as a Savior, he was very dim. He ends up by saying that God will judge the world by Jesus. But men don't need to be judged so much as they need to be redeemed. It is for this that they hunger and thirst. Paul said to the intellectual elite of Athens that God will judge the earth by this Jesus. What the world needed was not judgment; it needed redemption.

Paul did not emphasize redemption. He left Athens a comparative failure for he wrote no letter to the philosophers, a letter he could have written if there had been someone to write to. Apparently Paul's visit to Athens was a blur. It left no mark, only a blur, and so he went to Corinth a very chastened man. He said to the Corinthians, "I decided to know nothing among you except Jesus Christ and him crucified." (I Cor. 2:2). Jesus Christ was the total answer, and crucified, the total redemption. The consequence is that Paul left letters to the Corinthians that changed the world. So while Paul seemed to fail in one place, he was redemptive in another.

Of all the thirsts that men and women have, the thirst to be different from what they are is perhaps supreme. Men have pursued this even to the point of reaching for divinity. A certain mountain in Japan is a good example. The search there is to get rid of the problems of life. This mountain is so holy, according

55

to legend, that there can be no birth, no marriage, and no death there, because these three speak of the presence of man. The presence of man spoils everything. This is the supreme attempt to escape the inescapable realities of human existence. It is No to human nature —with a vengeance! It is a sweeping No, keeping all the problems away by keeping all the persons away. It is fear become dominant The ancient Greeks pursued a similar course on the holy island of Delos.

Another attempt at satisfying ultimate hungers and thirsts is to impose divine qualities upon human nature. In India there was a holy man who was thought to be the Incarnation. When asked if he were, he said, "No, I'm a sinner." The claim from being God to being a sinner was a great descent. The attempt to try to be God ended in hopelessness.

The attempts of man to be different by becoming God have been, and ever shall be, a distinct and definite failure. It hasn't happened and ought not to happen. The attempt of man to deify himself adds up to a zero and ever shall end up in a zero. Man can never become God. It is a complicated business of running the universe. It is too complicated for man's thought, body, and energy. We haven't ever succeeded, and we cannot.

Any plan to bridge the gap between God and man will be done by God on his terms We believe it has happened. Apart from Jesus Christ, I have never seen one or ever heard of one. Every claim to be God has always resulted in the weird, but never in the adequate.

This attempt to be God always used to show its bankruptcy at our Round Table Conferences in India.

There we gathered together the best representatives of every religious community. We did so for over fifty years. We asked them not to argue or try to make a case, but rather tell what they had actually found in religious experience. After fifty years I have never seen anyone who ever said or left the impression that he or she had actually found God or the Son of God by their own efforts and initiatives. Every Round Table Conference for half a century ended up in the same place: everything has been pushed to the edges, except Jesus Christ. Where he has been emphasized as the Way, a satisfying experience of God is almost universal. On the philosophical side Eastern religions are wonderful. On the experimental and experiential side, they are close to nil, except for those who came into contact with Jesus Christ. This isn't dogmatism. It is a proven fact by countless experiences of interreligious dialogue in India, the world's greatest laboratory of living religions.

The facts are throwing us into the arms of Christ for a new birth, for we are lost if a new birth doesn't happen. I believe that is an open door. The Divine Yes is Yes that we can be changed, and changed now in this birth! The answer is new birth in this life. It is a workable proposition if we come to Jesus Christ, so we turn to it expectantly. Those who hunger and thirst for righteousness shall indeed be filled.

Is There a Way of
Affirming One's Self?

Is there a way of affirming one's self? Yes, by deny-
ing one's self. Paradoxically, we find ourselves by giving ourselves away. God builds the bridge between
himself and man. We cross the gap between God and
man by self-surrender to God. This means that God remains God and we remain persons, but heightened
persons, different persons. Heightened persons because of laying hold of heightening power; different
persons because we are laying hold of different power.
This leaves God as God and man as man, a very different man when surrendered to God.

Self-surrender is the way out of being what we are
into being what we might be and ought to be. The
way of self-surrender works with an almost mathematical precision. One lady said to me, "I've found you
out. You have only one remedy—self-surrender." I
laughed and said, "I'm glad you found me out, for I
have found myself out." I can't go down the road with
any person about anything without running into the
problem of the unsurrendered self. It is the basis of all
our human problems. The surrendered self is the open
door to the solution to all our problems.

A woman said to me, "It is so comfortable to get
yourself off your own hands and into the hands of
God." It is not only comfortable, but comfortable in
the original sense of that term—com "with" and fortis
"strength"—"strengthened by being with." You are
strengthened with all the power of the higher Power. It

is a transfusion that makes us become a transformed person, different—doing things that you can't do and going places that you can't go and being what you can't be.

Jesus said, "Truly, truly, I say to you, unless a grain of wheat falls into the earth and dies, it remains alone; but if it dies, it bears much fruit." (John 12:24). Here he lifted up a principle at the very heart of the universe and by it shows the Divine Yes, the very center of life. It is yes that becomes no, that loses its life and finds it again.

I have said elsewhere that Thomas Huxley once wrote to Charles Kingsley and said that the attitude of the scientist is complete surrender to the will of God. Science says, "Sit down before the facts as a little child. Give up every preconceived notion. Be willing to be led to whatever end nature will lead you or all you will know is nothing." Science and the Christian faith each teach complete surrender. Science says, "Surrender to the facts." The Christian faith says, "Surrender to God, the Fact." One says, "Surrender to facts" and the other says, "Surrender to Fact," capital F.

Self-surrender is the secret of life. When you know that you know everything of significance. Fail that, and you fail everything. But man hasn't learned that. He is trying to save his life and loses it. Every self-centered person is an unhappy person. He does what he likes, but then he doesn't like what he does. He saves his life and then he loses it. A psychiatrist said that it is one hundred chances to one that the self-centered are unpopular. With whom? With themselves. They

59

center themselves on themselves and then life turns sour on their hands.

If a grain of wheat falls into the ground and dies it brings forth much fruit. It is wheat multiplied. It is creative energy. If you refuse to die to yourself, you won't have any self to die to.

A very prominent pastor would hug himself while he was preaching, a symbol of what he was doing inwardly. He was his own idol, but the idol had feet of clay. The consequence was that he did what this verse says: "He abides by himself alone." The punishment is in the person. When we center on ourself, we have self-punishment. The law of life is to lose your life. Disobey that law and you break yourself upon it.

What happens when we limit our life by self-surrender? Are we canceled? No, just the opposite. The specific problem that was facing Jesus was self-surrender. In this context the Greeks who came to see him didn't just come for an interview. They came to invite him to come to Greece to be their honored teacher, to put his philosophy into Greek culture, and thus spread it throughout the world. They saw if he went on to Jerusalem, it meant the opposite. They would crucify him. The Greeks came to invite him out of Jerusalem to Athens to save his life and live long. He would be honored, respected and loved in the Greek world. To go to Jerusalem with its fanatics would mean he would lose his life. But Jesus saw the difference. Jerusalem would be self-giving and world-finding while Greece would be self-finding, but world-losing. Every person faces that problem. More people trip over that problem into nonentity than over any other question.

Some people think if you surrender to Christ, you surrender to being canceled out. Canceled? All you think and act and are become heightened by the heightened contact. Everything happens "after" for it is the same surrender that ink makes to an author. Mere coloring matter becomes words that burn and bless and heighten. It is the same surrender that a wire makes to a dynamo. Unattached, it has no light or power, but surrendered to the dynamo, it throbs with light and power not its own. When you surrender to Jesus Christ a plus is added to all you do and think and are. You do the things you can't do and are a person you cannot be otherwise.

Charles Wesley wrote, "He speaks, and listening to his voice,/New life the dead receive." This has been verified among millions wherever it has been tried. He speaks, and listening to his voice, a society woman came alive: "New life the dead receive." She said to me, "If I had what you have, I wouldn't be in the mess that I am in." Her life was in a mess. Her home was to break up after Christmas, and she had no inner resources to meet that impending tragedy. I said, "My sister, if you will surrender yourself to Christ, you'll have the answer." She said she would try but didn't know how.

Then she wrote a letter to God in the language of the country club, which was the only language she knew, saying this, "Dear God, life has dealt me a bad hand. I don't know what card to lead. Show me which card to lead, and I'll lead it." A dim prayer, but profoundly meant and God heard it. Her home did not break up after Christmas. Her changed life held it together, and now I believe she is the best speaker on the home I know of. The denomination to which she belongs made her vice-president of all its missionary work at home and abroad, the highest office that could be given to a woman in that denomination at that time. A score of years ago her life was a mess; now it is a message, and what a message! "And listening to his voice, new life the dead receive." The dead become alive wherever human beings come in contact with that life. Jesus was and is the Divine Yes to a nobody who became a somebody!

He speaks and listening to his voice, a Wall Street broker responded. I was asked to speak at a luncheon party to all the bankers of Wall Street. At the close of the meeting a prominent broker said to me, "Where do you go next?" I told him. He said, "I want to take you in my car." He had scarcely gone a block, when he turned to me and said, "How do you get the thing you were talking about?" I asked him whether we could talk about it while going through the traffic of that city. He said, "There's no other place." I said, "You watch the traffic and I'll talk." I told him how he had to give himself in self-surrender, and when I got to the place where I thought he was ready, I asked him if we could pray going along. He said, "I'd like you to pray, but I'll have to watch the traffic." I'm not sure but what I kept my own eyes open! But we were borne up into God's help, for God was waiting for him to "hear his voice" and come to him in self-surrender and acceptance. When I jumped out of the car to go to my next appointment, he grabbed my hand in his and said, "Thank you. I'm in!" And he was! The Divine Yes had affirmed his life.

I was holding the National Christian Mission

throughout America under the auspices of the Federal Council of Churches, and in Minneapolis, Minnesota, as a part of that mission we had a meeting of the government officials of the State of Minnesota. I said to as a part of that mission we had a meeting of the government service, they should start with the same sense of Christian vocation and dedication as a Christian minister should show in his churchly ministry. Judge Youngdahl was in the audience as a listener, and he said to himself while I was talking, "Why should I not give up the security of the supreme court judgeship and run for governor?" He made the decision then and there and went on three times to win the election for governor and to clean up the public life of the state of Minnesota.

I was talking to a bishop who had retired. He was frustrated. When he was no longer in the limelight of the bishopric, he was frustrated and told me so. He wanted to know the secret of victorious living. I told him it was in self-surrender. The difference was in giving up the innermost self to Jesus. The difference was in the texture of the things that held him. When the outer strands were broken by retirement, the inner strands were not enough to hold him. Apparently he had a case of "limelight-itis" instead of a case of surrender to Jesus. Fortunately, with me, surrender to Jesus was the primary thing, and when the outer strands were cut by this stroke, my life didn't shake.

They say in Switzerland that the Swiss climbers have a rope, the strands of which at the center are the strongest and are capable of holding up a man even if all the edges of the rope have worn off. The inmost strands are the strongest. I have found that to be true

63

in Christian experience. Many of the strands of my life have been broken by this stroke, for I can no longer preach and I cannot write as my eyesight is so poor that I cannot see my own writing. I can only dictate into a tape recorder. The things that were dear to me, for the time being, are broken. The innermost strands belonging to the Kingdom and the Person of Jesus and my experience of him holds me as much as the total rope, for the innermost strands are the strongest. I need no outer props to hold up my faith, for my faith holds me. Though I do not possess my faith, it possesses me.

Jesus is the Divine Yes to human change wherever it is tried and seriously worked out. An African, after surrendering himself to Christ, changed his name, calling himself, "After." All the important things that happened in his life began to happen after surrendering his life to Christ and moving up into the power of Christ. To affirm ourselves we deny ourselves.

Is There a Way of Beginning Again?

How often do we wish we could start all over again. Here is a persistent thing in the human heart. Is there a way of beginning again? The Christian testimony is unanimous in its answer: Yes. And what we long for, Jesus Christ, the Divine Yes, affirms.

This deep experience is the most beneficial thing. Human nature and human character can be changed by conversion. It is the very nature of human nature to change.

A young man decided he would give up the Christian faith and try the way of sin and do everything in the book that was unchristian. He wanted to see whether he belonged to this life of sin. At the end of a year, he wrote to a friend saying, "Please help me to come home!" Goodness was home; sin was foreign. The young man thought that sin was natural, and that the Christian way made you out of step with everybody else in the universe. He read in one of my books that the Christian way was the natural way, and that sin and evil were unnatural. He doubted the fact, but he was wrong. When he was a Christian, the sum total of reality was standing behind him, reinforcing him. The young man thought that being a Christian was out of step with the universe. Sitting in a restaurant, he surrendered to Christ. When he left the restaurant, he was clapping his hands in tune with nature. The trees were clapping their hands, nature was in tune with him, and the sum total of reality was behind him. Nevermore would he feel "not at home" when he was a Christian. When we live this way, we have a sense of eternal belonging! We feel eternally at home. The Divine Yes had affirmed his significance with the gift of new life.

A man who was an alcoholic had a dog whom he loved very much. But one day when the dog jumped up in his lap and smelled his breath, he immediately turned around and jumped down. It struck the alcoholic very hard: even his pet dog had turned from him because of his alcoholism. He became a Christian because of the rejection of his dog, and from that time on the dog and he were the closest friends.

Another man told me that before he was converted, his dog never went to the front door with him when he left for work. But he always went to the front door when his wife left. It hurt him. He was converted, and the dog followed him to the door every morning and was there to greet him every evening. The dog knew the change that had taken place and that a new person had emerged. Even the dumb beasts sense genuine change.

Paul said, "The whole creation [all nature] is on tiptoe to see the wonderful sight of the sons of God coming into their own" (Rom. 8:19 Phillips). All plants know when you love them. The "green thumb" means the changed life. You can't raise animals or plants unless you love them. Love is the native air of the Kingdom. Therefore, things blossom and bloom under Christian love.

I once went to speak to the Rotary Club. I sat down alongside a Jewish Rabbi when I finished. I asked him, "Rabbi, was I too Christian for you today?" He said, "Oh, no. The more Christian you are, the better you'll treat the Jews!" Whether it is Jews or nature or yourself, the Christian way is the natural way to live, and you find you are in your homeland the moment you become Christian.

No wonder Jesus said that you must be born again, or born from above. This shows that the new birth is not an adopted doctrine of the Church, but a message and a fact delivered by Jesus to the Church. A real Christian ought to be born again. It is not something to believe in, but something to find and experience and propagate. Someone asked George Whitefield why he preached so much on the new birth. He preached on it three hundred times. He replied, "Because you **must** be born again." It was not a doctrine to be preached. It was a fact to be experienced and propagated.

The conservative groups divide people into "born again" Christians and the once born. Really you are not a Christian when you merely believe in the new birth, but rather when you have experienced the facts of new birth. I was in no sense a Christian except in clinging precariously to the fringes of the movement until I experienced the new birth. I had been seeking for three days. I was lifting up my hands to the skies for some handclasp from the Divine but none came. Then before I went to the church that Sunday night, I knelt beside my bed and prayed, "Oh, Lord, please save me tonight!" Expectancy had come into it and I, for the first time, had some ray of hope in my heart. A light had pierced my darkness. He was going to do it! My eagerness to get to the church made me run the mile from my home to the church, for I was taught you were saved on your knees at an altar of prayer.

Once there I went to the front row of seats in the church, hoping the speaker would get through his address quickly so that I could implement it and find the new birth. He had scarcely given the invitation to come to the altar, when I found I was the first one there. I had hardly touched my knees to the floor when Heaven flooded me with assurance. The universe opened its arms and said that I was accepted. My darkness turned to light. I grabbed the shoulders of the man kneeling beside me and said to him, "I've got it!" "It"—but it was really a "him." I had him and he had me, and we had each other. I was born again! I felt like I wanted to put my arms around the world and share this with everybody.

Seventy-one years have gone by since then, but I still want to put my arms around the world and share this with everybody. At eighty-eight I am just as eager to share this with everybody, even if I have to do it now from a wheelchair in a rehabilitation hospital. I was reborn before the stroke, and I am still reborn after the stroke. Nothing has altered this reality for I am centrally saved and safe. I hope my last days will be spent in saying, "I commend my Savior to you!" Life for me is before Christ (B.C.) and after Christ (A.C.). Before and after new birth. There is nothing the same except my name.

I was near the bottom of my class when I was converted, and I said, "This is no place for a Christian." I moved up toward the top. I needed something to bring all life into coherence, meaning, and goal. And Jesus was that something. He was the Divine Yes that brought all conflicting "No's" into coordination and goal.

Fortunately, I put my hand into the hand of Christ early in life, and this saved me from many things that would have led me astray. It was at age seventeen that I gave my life to Christ. At twenty-three I was asked by a college president to come and teach in his college. He said, "It is the will of the student body, the will of the townspeople, the will of the faculty, and we believe it is the will of God for you to teach in this college." At the same time I had a letter from a very trusted friend who said, "I believe it is the will of God for you to go into evangelistic work here in America." At the same time I had a letter from the Methodist Board of Missions saying, "It is our will to send you to India." At the time I was myself impressed that it was

God's will for me to go as a missionary to Africa—a call then generally supposed to be tantamount to a death warrant.

Here was a perfect traffic jam of wills. I went to my room, got on my knees and said, "Lord I am willing to go anywhere and do anything you want me to do." I asked him to tell me his will, and I would obey. The answer came back, "It's India." I said Yes, and there were no question marks. I knew. I never raised the question of whether a missionary got a salary or not. I never knew until I received my first month's salary of $50 how much it would be. I felt that "if God guides, God provides." I found it to be true then and true now. I have never wanted for anything that I have needed.

Fifty years later I knelt before him again, in the same room where I got my first call, and I said, "Lord, thank you for telling me fifty years ago that it was India. Give me my life choices to make over again, and I would make them as I have made them, with this proviso that where I have been untrue, I would be true. You have never let me down. I have let you down, but you have never let me down." And that was after fifty years of testing, and it includes the testing of this stroke.

My granddaughter said to me, "Granddaddy, if you had your choices to make over again, would you make them as you have made them, if this stroke were a part of it?" I replied, "Ann, not only would I do it once, I would do it many times." She said, "How many times?" I said, "Name the number and I would guarantee to do it." He has never let me down, and he has never been less than I wanted him to be. He has al-

The Divine Yes

ways been a surprise, and stroke or no stroke, I am his and will be forever. I did not follow him because I had no stroke. I followed him because "by his stripes I am healed."

One of the greatest things General William Booth, founder of the Salvation Army, ever did occurred, when after an eye operation he was told by his son, "Father, I am afraid you will never see my face again." Booth said, "Do you mean I will never see your face again?" The son replied, "Well, that seems to be it." The old general leaned over and stroked the face of his dear son and said, "Son, I served God and the people with my eyes, and I will serve God and the people with my blindness." No more noble words could be said.

Dr. Starbuck, the famous psychiatrist, said that every life is stunted unless it receives the metamorphosis called conversion. If the church allows this experience to fossilize, then psychology, when it becomes truly biological, will preach it. Indeed, the chief fact in genetic psychology is conversion, a change of momentous and scientific importance and interest. He says that without this every life is stunted, with no exceptions, East or West, North and South.

Dag Hammarskjöld, General Secretary of the United Nations was one of the ablest of men. In his memoirs, Markings, there is an entry on Whitsunday, 1961—that is, Pentecost—just four months before his tragic death in a plane crash in Africa. I quote:

"I don't know Who—or what—put the question. . . . I don't even remember answering. But at some moment I did answer Yes to Someone—or Something—and from that hour I was certain that existence is meaningful and that, therefore, my life, in self-surrender, had a goal."[1]

He had said Yes to the Divine Yes.

Then there is Srinavasa Shastri, one of the greatest and noblest of India's sons, head of a great university and the Servants of India Society. I asked him once, "Mr. Shastri, do you partake of the skepticism of Poona?" Poona was the most skeptical part of India. He replied, "I am not religious, but I am not irreligious. I'm not religious because it is not real to me. I wish it were for I have no divine spark to give to the movement which I head, The Servants of India Society. My heart is ashes. How did it become real to you?" So then and there I told him of my conversion. He replied, "Now I see what I need. I need conversion. Either I must be converted on my own and for myself, or else I must warm my heart against somebody's heart that has been converted."

The best man that ever lived said: You must be born again if you are to see the Kingdom of God. So it is not merely right, it is "good news" that men can be born again. But the question is often raised, Can a man live without being born again? Can he get along pretty well without being born again? The answer is, Can the lungs get along pretty well without air? Can the eye get along without light? Can the heart get along without love? If so, we can get along pretty well without Jesus Christ and his new birth.

On the international level and local political level

---

[1] Dag Hammarskjöld, **Markings**, trans. Leif Sjöberg and W. H. Auden (New York: Alfred A. Knopf, 1964), p. 205.

The Divine Yes

the pressure for moral and spiritual conversion is the same. The world situation is ripe for the Kingdom of God. Conversion has become a political necessity as well as a moral and spiritual necessity until at last the Divine Yes sounds in political halls, as well as in the experience of ordinary men and women.

Is There a Continuing Divine Presence?

We come now to the center of the Divine Yes, this Living Christ. Is it possible for this Living Christ to live within us? Yes!—through the Holy Spirit who is the applied edge of redemption. Without the Holy Spirit the Christian faith is an "outwardism," and "outwardism" is one of the things that Jesus fought against most severely. It resulted in Phariseeism. Again I say the Holy Spirit is the applied edge of redemption. Everything that Jesus did and taught and was becomes applied in us by the Holy Spirit. Somehow the Holy Spirit has not been adequately emphasized in Christian service. Without the Holy Spirit Christian responsibility is a burden; with the Holy Spirit it is a blessing.

Many Christians work under the power of their own resolutions in the demands of duty. They do not have or allow the power of the Holy Spirit to work in them and for them. The Holy Spirit is the crux of Pentecost. But the Holy Spirit could not be given until Jesus had been glorified. Jesus had to live, teach, die, and illustrate the meaning of the Holy Spirit before the Holy Spirit could be given in power.

The Old Testament account says, "The Spirit of the

72

Lord came mightily upon him [Samson] . . . [and he went out] and slew a thousand men therewith" (Judg. 15:14-15 KJV). Now put that into the pages of the New Testament and see how it sounds: "The Holy Spirit came upon the one hundred and twenty in the Upper Room after Pentecost and they went out and slew a thousand men who had slain Jesus." We shudder at the idea. Why? Jesus had to put his own character content into the Holy Spirit. He was God in flesh and the Holy Spirit is a person like Jesus. "The [Holy] Spirit had not been given, because Jesus had not yet been glorified" (John 7:39 NEB). Why couldn't the Holy Spirit be given until Jesus had been glorified? Because the life of Jesus had to be the norm of the Holy Spirit. Because Jesus and the Holy Spirit had to become actual in the lives of the followers of Jesus. Jesus was the embodiment and illustration of the Holy Spirit.

Peter said, in regard to what happened at the Gentiles' Pentecost at the house of Cornelius, "God who knows the heart bore witness to them, giving them the Holy Spirit just as he did to us; and he made no distinction between us and them, but cleansed their hearts" (Acts 15:8-9). He said there was no difference between the Jews' Pentecost (Acts 2) and the Gentiles' Pentecost (Acts 10) in that they both received the Holy Spirit and had their hearts purified by faith. Purity of heart is a permanent element in the midst of the gifts of the Holy Spirit. Do we need that? Look into your own heart and get the answer. We all need it.

The first thing about the experience of the Holy Spirit is that this extends to the subconscious mind, so now the total person, conscious and subconscious, is subject to the control of the Holy Spirit. Therefore he or she becomes a person purified by the Holy Spirit. He is not subject to whims and notions but is now subject to the Holy Spirit who holds the citadel and guides him from within. In other words, the inner life has been taken over by the Holy Spirit who keeps the whole life steady and is not subject to ups and downs. He keeps us surrendered. We don't sit on a lid. We trust him and he keeps us victorious. The Christian life is one of trust and rest—not struggle under our own power.

The second factor that seems to be permanent is this: Jesus said, "You shall receive power when the Holy Spirit has come upon you; and you shall be my witnesses in Jerusalem and in all Judea and Samaria and to the end of the earth!" (Acts 1:8). Here it says that something will be persistent to the ends of the earth; namely, power to witness to Jesus. That was the power to witness to Jesus effectively. Now note this is not just power, a power to perform miracles, but the power to witness to Jesus effectively, and that is the kind of power we all need. Without it, we preach dead truth, but with it we preach spirit-quickened, living truth.

So two things are permanent at Pentecost—purity for ourselves and power to impart the Message to others. Do we need those two things? Nothing is more necessary than to have purity to settle our own problems, and power to impart this gift to other people. One for myself and the other for the other person. Nothing could be more necessary and all-inclusive. He is not only the principle and power, but the instant he breathes on us we become resurrection, for we have the Spirit of Resurrection—the Holy Spirit.

We should take note of the change a modern translation makes. Where the King James version of the Bible says, "Be filled with the Spirit," the New English Bible reads, "Let the Holy Spirit fill you" (Eph. 5:18 NEB). In other words, we don't have to be filled with the Holy Spirit by our own efforts; we now have to consent for him to fill us. The initiative is his. He is our Divine Initiative. All we have to do is to say Yes to the Divine Yes, and we will be filled with the Spirit. Therefore, the idea of storming heaven to get into fellowship with the Holy Spirit is wrong. We don't have to overcome his reluctance, but lay hold of his highest willingness. We have just to say Yes to his Yes and creation begins anew and we are filled with the Spirit.

Breath control, as in Yoga, is the human answer to improve yourself by regulating your breath. But Jesus said something else. He breathed on them and said, "Receive ye the Holy Spirit." It was not breath control, but receiving the very breath of God, the Spirit of God. It is a Person that we receive. The wonder of it is receiving the Holy Spirit, not passively receiving, but actively receiving. So ths Divine Yes is really saying, "Take ye the Holy Spirit." Not a human manipulation of our breath, but a divine acceptance of the very breath of God—the breath that breathed upon chaos and out of it came cosmos. Whenever we say Yes to him we enter cosmos out of chaos. In any situation, in anything, he is cosmos instead of chaos. Sin is chaos and acceptance of the Holy Spirit is cosmos. Wherever Jesus is, he is creation. In Jesus, Yes: out of nothingness—everything comes.

Moffatt translates from the Bible in this way: "I am myself resurrection and life" (John 11:25). Where Jesus is, there is not only the resurrection, the resurrected Lord, but he is resurrection. He is not only resurrected; he is resurrection! He is the Spirit and Power of the Resurrection. Wherever he is, there is resurrection. So when he breathed on them, he was saying: Receive resurrection. Receive the principle (Spirit) and the power. Here is a supreme affirmation of life—in the face of death. Divine Yes? Indeed!

Are There Gifts of the Spirit?

I would not have written this section if this were not a problem to many present-day Christians. Are there gifts of the Holy Spirit? Is it necessary for the Spirit-filled Christian to speak in tongues? The first question must be answered affirmatively. There are, indeed, spiritual gifts. Paul mentions them several times—I Corinthians 12-14, Romans 12, Ephesians 4. Though some Christians in the first century and in our own speak in tongues, this is by no means a requirement or a necessary sign of being filled with the Spirit. Tongues were a problem in the Corinthian church, and they are today. Sometimes it is urged that you have the Holy Spirit if you have the gift of tongues; otherwise, there is no Holy Spirit.

Incidentally, this discussion of tongues contained in I Corinthians 12 through 14 is the only mention of tongues in the whole of the epistles of Paul, John, Peter, and all the rest of the epistles, with the possible exception of one reference in Romans 8. And the subject was only raised in these three chapters because it was causing division and confusion. In all the theological writings of the apostles it is only mentioned once. If it has the importance now being given to it in certain quarters, why was it not mentioned more than this once? They mention "love, joy, and peace" again and again and again—the gift of tongues once. So the gift of tongues was not the working emphasis in the early church.

The New Testament distinguishes the gift (singular) of the Spirit, fruits of the Spirit, and gifts of the Spirit (plural). The gift of the Spirit is the heritage of every baptized and converted Christian. If we are utterly open to him, we are filled with the Holy Spirit. Flowing out of this fact, there are inevitably fruits of the Spirit. The gifts of the Spirit are given according to the will of God—for the upbuilding of the whole Christian community.

There were two types of tongues which are spoken of in the Acts of the Apostles. One is connected with Pentecost (Acts 2), and the other is connected with Corinth and the Corinthians (I Cor. 12-14). The apparent reason for the tongues connected with Pentecost is this. There was a moot question in the churches that if you became a Christian, you would also have to become a Jew, adopt their culture, and their language. God broke that pattern. Men from that ancient world —Asia, Africa, Europe—heard the apostles speaking to every man in his own language. They looked at each other and said, "Why, he is speaking in our language"; a second said, "They are speaking in our language"; the third said, "Why they are speaking in our language." Every man heard in his own language the wonderful works of God.

This meant the universalizing of the Gospel. It was rather like the Tower of Babel episode in reverse. God was going to use every language, every culture, every nation. The language barrier was down. This first happened in Jerusalem, the center of the Hebrew language (Acts 2:5), then again in Caesarea, a Roman center of the Latin language (Acts 10:46). The third time it occurred in Ephesus, a center of the Greek language (Acts 19:6). These were the three languages that were used at the cross: Hebrew, Latin, and Greek. Now this was peculiar and it was a special miracle to show that the Gospel is universalized. God was using all languages, for the men who heard at Pentecost needed no interpreter. They heard directly in the language they used, their own. This was a special miracle to universalize the Gospel. It is set forth dramatically by Luke.

As far as I know, this has never been repeated. It is unique. In India people have come thinking they could speak directly in the language of the people without an interpreter and without learning the language. The wreckage of those hopes have been strewn across India. It hasn't happened. There is no clearly authenticated instance of this, though the claim has often been made.

The kind of "speaking in tongues" that is manifested today is the Corinthian type and needs interpretation as it is unknown to the speaker and to the hearer, "unless there is someone to do the interpretation." The need to have someone who can interpret the unknown tongue introduces another mediator between man and

God. The New Testament says "there is one Mediator"
—Jesus. But how do I know the interpreter isn't intro-
ducing his own thoughts and calling them the word of
God? It would be dependent on whether the interpreter is truly inspired of God. If not, then it could be
something entirely different. Moreover, this must be
said: only where it is taught that tongue-speaking ac-
companies the coming of the Holy Spirit does this
phenomenon occur. Paul counseled against it, as being
one of the lower gifts of the Spirit.

While some sages are quite sure that Jesus never
spoke in tongues, he nevertheless said the apostles
would speak in tongues: "These signs will accompany
those who believe: in my name they will cast out de-
mons; they will speak in new tongues; they will pick
up serpents, and if they drink any deadly thing, it will
not hurt them; they will lay their hands on the sick,
and they will recover" (Mark 16:17-18). If those five
things were a permanent part of Pentecost, the coming
of the Holy Spirit, a kind of esoteric religion would
have resulted. It would mean magical or semimagical
power for not one of those five things mentioned is a
moral quality. Every one of them is a semimagical
quality.

Had the Christian faith gone across the world with
those five things upon its banners, it would have died
among the magic and mystery cults, for not one of
them is a moral quality. The Christian faith would
have turned from morals to magic and would have
died in the process. The passage where these five
things were mentioned seems not to be a part of the
Gospel, for the last verses of Mark are highly suspect
as they varied in the early texts. They were second-

and third-century attempts to fill out the Gospel of
Mark, which was evidently lost from the eighth verse
of the sixteenth chapter. They represent exactly the
kind of a list a man unaided by divine inspiration
would make out.

If you take any one of those five things, you have to
take them all, including picking up deadly serpents
and drinking any deadly thing. But you say, Paul
picked up a deadly serpent when he was shipwrecked
on the island of Malta. Yes, in gathering sticks Paul
accidentally picked up a serpent that fastened on his
hand, (Acts 28:3). He shook it into the fire and no
harm came to him. It was in the line of duty as a
Christian. But suppose Paul had said to the Maltese:
"Do you want to see what kind of people we are? Got
any snakes around here? Let them bite us." If Paul
had done that he would have died, for he would have
been something counter to the Gospel. Signs and
wonders would be the business of the Holy Spirit instead of changed moral character. So the Christian
faith would have turned from a redemptive, moral and
spiritual movement to a wonder cult, showing semimagical powers as a sign of a moral movement. It
would have died, and it should have died had it been
dependent on that!

We have seen that there are two permanent things
in Pentecost: purity and power. They are as vital
today as they were in those days. They are not evi-
dence of a "showman's religion." The genius of the
Christian faith is seeing today that wherever the use of
tongues is made as a sign of the gift of the Holy Spirit,
you will find inevitable division. It did so then and
does so now. The fruits of the Spirit do not divide;

they unite (Gal. 5:22). We cannot have too much of love, joy, peace, and the other fruits of the Spirit.

We welcome those who speak in tongues to have fellowship in the Ashram movement, provided they speak tongues to themselves and do not make it a public issue. In the New Testament tongues were intended as an aid to private prayer and not as an evangelistic method. We accept those who speak them because they belong to Christ, not because they speak in tongues or do not speak in tongues. We both belong to Christ, of whom there is no record that he spoke in tongues. It is possible to have the gift of the Spirit without gifts of the Spirit.

It is a fact that people who receive the gifts of the Holy Spirit with the accompaniment of tongues are often profoundly changed morally. The change may come through the acceptance of the Holy Spirit with the accompaniment of tongues, but the tongues may be a divisive element and may have nothing to do with the change of moral character.

When you receive the gift of the Holy Spirit, with or without the accompaniment of tongues, you change people by that experience. But the change can be accounted for by the fact that they received the gift of the Holy Spirit and not the accompanying gift of tongues. The Holy Spirit is the person who changes them, not the tongues. The gift of tongues is a rider which has nothing to do with the immense power and heightened moral and spiritual life of the recipient. It is the Holy Spirit that made them different because they received him. The gift of tongues can be a liability rather than an asset. It may have harmed as many as it has converted. Wisely St. Paul said, "Earnestly desire the higher gifts" (I Cor. 12:31), which God distributes according to his pleasure for the good of the whole Church.

Our pattern of the Spirit-filled person must be Jesus. We would be filled with the Spirit and be made like him. He is the center of our unity and our pattern of the Spirit-filled life. He is Christ's continuing and continuous affirmation in us and through us.

Does Christianity Stand the Test?

Now comes the most important verse in all literature: For in him, at long last, the Divine Yes has sounded! Unless a supposed truth is put into life to see what life will do to it—prove it or disprove it—that supposed truth may continue to be a supposed truth, but not verified truth. The truth in Jesus is all verified truth, not the truths of a schoolmaster or philosopher. With him things come out of life, and when he speaks, he speaks to life. It is life verified, speaking to life wanting to be verified. He is, therefore, the leader of the Way. The Way is the Way that he himself has tried. Everything we face, he has also faced. His answer is the Answer of verified knowledge. It is deep speaking to deep and heart answering heart. The things that he verified are not merely piddling things, but vital in every one of life's circumstances. It is verified as important truth. It is as lasting as Eternity.

Does the Divine Yes speak only to the Church and Western civilization, or does it also speak universally? It seems clear that the Divine Yes is universal. It is, therefore, a word for our time, when human experience is becoming increasingly global. It has been my privilege to witness the Divine Yes sounding throughout the world.

In Japan the group called Democracy in Action (which is really Christianity in action) was started by Melvin Evans, one of our Ashram group. It was trying to change the relationship between capital and labor by changing the attitude of management. On a trip to Japan I met with some of these changed people. One of them, the head of a great electric firm, said, "My men are no longer mad at me because I am no longer mad at them." A change in management's attitude resulted in a change in labor.

A banker in Japan said to me, "Before the war they had a slogan in business that business is like a folding screen. You have to make it crooked to make it stand. If you make it straight, it won't stand." So they said that business wouldn't work except through crookedness. They reported further that the result was they had a very bad reputation in Japan for their goods which were shoddy goods.

They decided to change this basic slogan in business and put in one closer to the Christian's: "Thou shalt love thy neighbor as thyself," and "Do unto others as you would have them do unto you." The government appointed a special bureau to watch and see that everything that went out of Japan conformed to those two maxims or the goods were not allowed to be shipped. The result was that the Japanese reputation for integrity and honesty and high quality goods went up, up near the top. The Japanese economists and businessmen discovered that the Christian way in business was the workable way. Good business affirms; it does not negate.

I was talking to the ex-headhunters of Borneo who lived in one of the big longhouses. I stood under a cluster of twenty-four human skulls owned by the member of the house. He said, "Christianity is the only religion where you can't wangle God to get gifts out of him. You have to obey his laws. Then, and then only, can you get anything out of him." This from an ex-headhunter who is now a Christian! The Divine Yes is sounding even to the headhunters because it belongs.

Some of the followers of Vivekananda, a great leader in the World Parliament of Religion held in Chicago just prior to the turn of the century, were talking together about various things and they began to talk about Christ and his sacrifice upon the cross. They said, "Why can't we do that?" Out of that question the Rama Krishna Mission was organized. It put sacrificial service into India. It was organized on Christmas Eve, so they meet on Christmas Eve to commemorate the founding of that movement. It was the most vital movement among non-Christians, among the Hindus of India, who received inspiration from the Cross and Jesus. So the Yes is sounding beyond the borders of the Christian faith. I predict when the Church and people outside the Church discover the Kingdom of God in the person of Jesus—the absolute Order and the absolute Person—we are going to have the greatest spiritual awakening that this planet has ever seen. It will all be around Jesus and his Message. Nothing else works. This does!

Christian truth must be tested in the crucible of life. I believe God is saying to me, "I am handing you back your life for a demonstration period at the very end, so that a viewer looking on may see if there is anything in it." I can't afford to be anything but grateful that he thought enough of me to give me this period at the end of life to be a proof that what I've spoken about—the unshakable Kingdom and the unchanging Person—is true because I'm showing it to be true by his Grace.

"The divine 'yes' has at last sounded in him, for in him is the 'yes' that affirms all the promises of God." This verse says that at long last Jesus is come to be the verification. At "long last" points to the fact that mankind waited for ages for Jesus to come. All nations have had some "intimation" of the word "come." Hinduism speaks of ten avatars ("descents" or "incarnations") of divinity—among them the most familiar are Rama and Krishna. So far nine have appeared and they await the tenth, a spotless incarnation, without blame or blemish still to come. We believe he has come and we are proclaiming what the nations have desired, consciously or unconsciously, in Jesus! So the nations will feel that it is a "home-coming" when they come to Jesus.

Long ago a Chinese engineer in Manchuria who had been in America for some years said to me, "What are you going to do with me? I am a man without a religion. I don't believe in Confucianism any more, and I don't believe that Jesus is divine, so none of the Christian churches will take me in. I am a man without a faith. What would you say to me?" I asked him how far he had come along. He replied, "I think that Jesus is the best man that ever lived." Then I said, "Jesus is your ideal?" "Yes," he replied, "he is." Then I said, "If he is the best of men and he is your ideal, you should take out of your life everything that contradicts that ideal." He replied, "That isn't easy." I said, "I didn't say it would be easy, but that it was necessary. If you are willing to do the will of God, you will know the will of God for he will teach you."

His face lighted up. He said, "Everybody else has said I had to believe something first, but you say if I were willing to do, I would know!" We prayed together that he might have power to surrender everything in his life that didn't conform to Jesus. He went home, but returned the next day all aglow. He said, "All my questions of who Jesus is have faded out in the night. I have felt and love the Presence. He has verified himself to me, and as I began to believe I began to know. I am so happy with it! I've been talking with my wife and she is coming to him also." So you don't have to encourage yourself to believe, but surrender and accept him as Savior and Lord.

These miracles are happening around the world, and happening with an almost mathematical precision. A divine precision takes place wherever Jesus is tried, and exposed to life, life lives itself again.

In Japan they told me the story of the evangelist who was holding a meeting and was staying with a doctor who was non-Christian. The doctor and his family didn't go to the meetings so when the evangelist returned from the meetings he would witness to them. They were interested, more than interested. They accepted it.

They were all baptized except the old mother. I say "old mother." She was only forty-five, but she was lying on her sick bed awaiting death. She had lived her life out at forty-five and felt she was too old to live longer. The evangelist went in and talked to her. She said, "No, I'm too old. I'm going to die." He asked her if she was ready to die and she said, "No." The evangelist said to her, "Your spirit is being held down to earth by your sins. Jesus will cut the ball and chain of sin that is holding you down to the earth and let your soul free to go to heaven." She said, "Oh, will he do that?" "Yes," he replied. She surrendered herself to Christ.

The next morning a strange thing happened. When she awoke she felt the impulse to look around. She said, "Look at the beautiful blossoms on the plum tree and that beautiful ant on the windowsill. I have never noticed them before. Aren't they beautiful? God made both of them!" She was so excited she wanted to get up from her bed. She crawled over to a chair and pulled herself up into it. She then began to go from chair to chair by herself. Her grandson took her on the back of his bicycle to call on her friends so that she could tell them what had happened to her. Soon it became a regular thing for them to go to call on her friends and tell them how resurrection had come into her life. All her old friends began to want to hear and know the secret of this woman's life. One day her grandson couldn't go so she walked to her friends. In her life the Divine Yes at long last had sounded.

Somebody asked a prominent Beirut official why there was such a failure of Christianity in the Near East. He answered it was because of "syncretism," the desire to be all things to all men and to be offensive to none. Man to affirm himself as God failed because he had nothing behind him but human affirmation.

87

The Divine Yes

Sister Lila, a very sympathetic Greek Orthodox nun, and a Hindu doctor went across India visiting the various Hindu ashrams and sacred places. They came back to Sat Tal, the original Christian Ashram of its type in India in the Himalayas, and said, "It is the twilight of the gurus. They will pass out of the picture as the Greek gods did in Greece in the twilight of the gods." The gurus have failed because they could not redeem the people who followed them. People looked to them, worshiped them and lauded them, but went away unchanged. They had no power to redeem human nature and make it different. It is all moonlight and not sunlight. It is decay.

An Indian lawyer who has visited several Hindu ashrams said, "I have sat at the feet of many gurus, worshiping them and lauding them, but I came back unchanged. They did not know how to redeem human nature. I came to Christ and everything is different."

Jesus Christ is the true guru, a Sanskrit word which means "dispeller of darkness." And who is this but the Divine Yes, the Light of the World.

The world is waiting for an affirmation on tiptoe, not only for a human affirmation, but for a divine affirmation as well. The divine affirmation, the Divine Yes, has at last sounded and if we affirm the Divine Yes, they will listen. We need both the human and the divine speaking the same thing.

Is the Divine Yes Addressed to Everyone?

We have endeavored to show that the Divine Yes appears to have a universal application. This should not surprise us for it is the "Gospel in miniature," as Luther called it, and addresses the whole world: "God so loved the world!" (John 3:16). But it is also addressed to everyone without any exception. It is my personal conviction that it is addressed to all, though, of course, there are those who will not or do not hear.

It needs to be reiterated that there seems to be a universal longing for what Christ offers. The pressure of the great need in our society for Christ is apparent everywhere. I told a friend from England that this pressure of necessity is being felt by the hippies to conquer drugs, sex, boredom, and frustration; that Jesus Christ is the only permanent answer to any and every problem in life and society. So this Jesus Revolution is proving the truth of the necessity of the world pressure. It is not going to lessen. It will increase.

In 1971 at Long Beach, California, I attended a meeting of seven thousand "hippies" identified with the Jesus movement. I thought the hippie movement was the most barren movement that ever struck America and one of the most dangerous. Their sex attitude was dissolving the moral and family life of the country. I picked up a hippie journal in Berkeley in which there were two hundred want ads: one hundred and sixty-five were for sex—men wanting men and women wanting women, women wanting men and men wanting women. Now the editor of that journal has been converted and is running a Christian journal. The most barren has become one of the most productive. The seven thousand ex-hippies were well behaved and were bursting with joy. They say that they can cure addiction in three minutes by surrender to Christ, and I believe it is true. This is not merely whis-

89

pered, it is sounded. The newspapers and magazines were forced to draw attention to this marvelous phenomenon that is sweeping across the younger generation who were the most riotous, but have now become one of the most righteous, forces of our generation. It has sounded, and it sounded from the housetops, and it is going on to older generations and catching on there.

All classes feel this deep necessity. One ancient papyrus, found in Egypt, has a supposed saying of Jesus: "Cleave the wood and thou shalt find Me; raise the stone and I am there." If we cleave the heart of modern man we shall find him in desire, perhaps not even known, but there just the same in a deep hunger of unsatisfaction, in a deep longing that is not merely written in the desire of man, but inwardly written in the depths of his person. He expresses it in many different ways, but he expresses it! Jesus is the Divine Yes that has at last sounded, and they will listen out of deep necessity.

It is not by chance that the song, "Amazing Grace, How Sweet the Sound," became so popular and was one of the best sellers in rock music, for it has an affinity with human need and human desire. This desire and need for Jesus Christ is not a passing mood or fad. It is a must in human relationships at the present time. Harvey Cox, a modern theologian, says that the hope for the arising of a future God is sustained by the nature of reality. He quotes an atheist in support of this.

The nature of things demands the rise of a future God. We believe that future God has risen and his face is the face of Jesus Christ and his head is crowned with thorns. We do not await him; he is already here.

Questions Which Demand an Affirmative Answer

When Peter asked Jesus, "Lord, to whom shall we go? You have the words of eternal life" (John 6:68), he said a profound thing. The inner cosmos was saying the same thing as the outer cosmos. So it registers itself in me as cosmic movement, and I have more and more cosmic backing. I have more of his cosmic spirit and joy. This descending phase is not listening to one's own verification, but walking to the music of the spheres. We need not have a sense of loneliness, but we may have a sense of "at-homeness" inwardly wherever we are.

A friend of mine said he couldn't accept Christ for he couldn't follow a loser. He felt that anyone who went to a cross was a loser. But when I follow Jesus, I am following a divine unshakable Kingdom and an unchanging Person who is the Divine Yes and saying it to the world's No. When you can use your enemies and make them further you, you know how to live, if not on account of, then in spite of. You are unbeatable. I have said No to my central ego and said Yes to his Central Ego, so I am a winner no matter what happens.

The fact is that in the direction of yes, towards the Divine Yes, one finds security. If the present generation begins to think and talk and act moral and spiritual regeneration, things are going to happen.

Perhaps the biggest hindrance to conversion is confounding it with proselytism. We need to join forces and together bring about a spiritual revolution that will change men and conditions. We need to go by the theory that if you belong to Christ and I belong to Christ, we belong to each other and should present a united front to the world. He is the Divine Yes that all men everywhere need and are seeking. If heaven lies about our infancy, the world lies about our middle age. Every man needs reconversion around forty to save him from the inroads of secularism and this world. A woman of our group said, "Include not only forty, but my age, seventy." More people die from the hardening of categories than they do from the hardening of their arteries.

An alcoholic came to a place of prayer and said, "O Jesus, if you are going to save me, why don't you do it?" Then he opened his eyes and claimed, "Boys, he has done it." Jesus is an open door. He was an open door to him and to everybody else. The Divine Yes had been addressed to him, and he'd heard. He no longer needed spirits, for he had the Spirit.

When one comes to Jesus, there is an awakening of the general personality. The Divine Yes can be seen in a woman in Africa who came to Christ, and she felt that she wanted to do something for Jesus. But she was blind an seventy years of age, and, therefore, her contributions did not seem to be very promising. She was uneducated, but she came to the missionary with her French Bible and said, "Would you mind underscoring John 3:16 in my Bible in red?" The missionary was very intrigued to see what she was going to do.

She took the French Bible and sat in front of a boys' school in the afternoon. When school was dismissed, she called these boys and said, "Boys come here please. Do you know French?" Very proudly they said that they did. Then she said, "Please read to me this passage underscored in red in my Bible." They did. Then she would ask, "What does this mean to you, boys?" They said, "We don't know." Then she said,

"I'll tell you what it means to me." And she told the story of the Gospel. Twenty-four young men became pastors or assistant pastors due to the work of that blind beggar. She was so transformed that people would call her "madame." She reached out and helped convert more than two dozen young people. She was no longer just a blind old woman; she was now a creative personality. The Divine Yes had sounded in her soul and remade her at seventy!

When we yield to him, we are not let down but lifted up. For the most exciting person in this universe is Jesus Christ with a surprise around every corner. Paul says, according to Moffatt's translation, "By all the stimulus of Christ" (Phil. 2:1). He said something very important. Jesus is the most stimulating person in this universe. We are not supposed to be excited when you reach the age of eighty-eight, but I am excited over Jesus. One of the most exciting things about the future is that, apparently, I will have more time to be with him! I always thought that when I reached the age when I could no longer travel that it would be very exciting to be shut up with him and the Bible. But now that I face him, not with ordinary need, but with extraordinary need, I find that I'm more and more going to be shut up with the loveliest and most beautiful and wisest person that ever lived.

This new appointment has been an appointment to live more closely and intimately, not with wise persons, but with the wisest Person that ever lived or ever shall live. So let no one pity me, but only congratulate me that I have an appointment day by day and hour by hour with the Son of God, who is the Son of Man and who loved me enough and trusted me enough to be the demonstration of the faith that I hold. Not many people have a chance to turn around at the end of life and tie up everything in demonstration knots. I am saying to the world, "This works!"

People often boast over their connections with the great. Here is an opportunity to be connected with the greatest. Jesus said, "He who receives you receives me, and he who receives me receives him who sent me" (Matt. 10:40). You are immediately in the presence of the greatest, God, and have a personal relationship with him. You are a somebody. You have become important by becoming one with the Highest in the universe. You have heard the Divine Yes.

Is There an Answer
to the Problem of Suffering?

We come now to the crux of this book, namely, Is Jesus the Divine Yes in a world of much unmerited suffering and pain? Is Jesus the Divine Yes at the place of unmerited suffering? This is perhaps the crux of the doubts of the modern man.

Each system of religious thought has claimed that it had the secret. All of them in order to exist in the real world thought they had to give some plausible answer.

The Stoics had an attitude that could be summed up in these words: "My head may be bloody, but it will be unbowed under the bludgeonings of chance." A noble creed and the attitude still persists in our literature; noble but very lacking. The Stoics in shutting out grief and sorrow also shut out love and pity. They apparently feared that unless you shut out love and

94

pity, all the world of grief and sorrow would troop in behind. But if you are a harsh, insensitive person lacking love, you are inadequate. So this is no answer.

Margaret Fuller once said, "I accept the universe." Carlyle's comment was: "God, she'd better!" There is nothing to do but to accept the things as they are, modified here and there.

When we turn to the ancient religious men and philosophers we find various answers. Buddha had the most radical of all. His was: As long as you are in life you are in sorrow. Cut the root of desire, even for life, and then you go out into the actionless, passionless state called Nirvana, the state literally of the snuffed-out candle. It is the vastest and most devastating No that has ever been said against life.

When we come to other non-Christian faiths, the answer in Hinduism is that there is no such thing as unmerited suffering. Whatever is, is just. Whatever suffering there is, is not unmerited. According to the Hindu law of Karma if you are suffering now, you have been sinful in this or in a previous birth. So there is no unmerited suffering.

A man in India said to me, "Jesus must have been a terrible sinner in a previous birth for he was such a terrible sufferer in this one." But I would suspect a premise that brought me to that conclusion. And yet it is the only conclusion the law of Karma would bring. Where there is suffering, there has to be sin, as suffering is the result of previous sin. They have a saying among the Hindus, "That just as a calf will find its mother among a thousand cows, so your sins will find you out among a thousand rebirths." So where there is suffering, there has been sin. It is all nonsense. The

Hindu has the spring of his compassion dried up by the law of Karma. If a man is suffering, it is because he has been sinful, and therefore you must let it take its course and not interfere with the law of Karma.

When we come to the Muslim attitude it is simple. Whatever happens is the will of God, and we must accept the will of God. All the good and evil that come upon us are alike his will, and we must submit to it. Islam means literally submission to the will of God. This concept is as stifling and stunting as it is static.

In the Old Testament there are two ways of thought in regard to unmerited suffering. One is that the righteous will be exempt from the things that fall upon the wicked. The thought is conveyed by these words: "Only with thine eyes shalt thou behold and see the reward of the wicked. . . . There shall be no evil befall thee, neither shall any plague come nigh thy dwelling" (Ps. 91:8, 10 KJV). The righteous will be exempt from the things that fall upon the wicked. There is a truth in that, of course, for the righteous know how to live in a world of this kind better than the wicked. They are not barking their shins upon the system of things. They know their way around better and are saved from many self-inflicted ills that fall upon those who break the moral law and are broken by it. But it is only a half-truth, for the righteous do suffer as other people and are not exempt from the sorrows that come from living. They get sick as other people and die as other people. So the prophet had difficulty in making these two ideas fit, namely, that if you are only good you will be exempt from the sorrow that hits other people. This was a point of puzzlement with the prophets.

Then there is the other train of thought in the Hebrew tradition as when the prophet said:

> Though the fig-tree may not
>   blossom,
> though no fruit is on the vine,
> though the olive crop has failed,
> though the fields give us no food,
> though the folds have lost their
>   flocks,
> and in the stalls no cattle lie,
> yet in the Eternal we will find
>   our joy,
> we will rejoice in the God who
>   saves us.
>   (Habakkuk 3:17 Moffatt)

This is very close to the New Testament idea. On the whole, though, we take the book of Job as a standard with respect to suffering for its ideas are congenial to us. Job was a righteous man undergoing more sorrows than other people. Nevertheless, he got three times as much back in the end, so he was paid back. It was a reward mentality. You got it here in this life if you kept your righteousness—three times as much as others.

There is no book of Job in the New Testament for the New Testament has a different point of view. The New Testament is quite different and unique. Two things strike us with surprise there. First of all, we are struck by the fact that Christ's attitude toward suffering is so different from that of others. And secondly, one is shocked by the fact that so few Christians have adopted Jesus' attitude toward suffering. He accepted the fact of human suffering. He neither explains it nor explains it away. If he had attempted to explain it, his message would have been merely another philosophy, for a philosophy has to have an explanation for everything. His was a gospel—Good News—even "in spite of." A philosophy explains, but it does not change. The Gospel may not explain, but it does utterly change. Jesus transforms suffering by using it. The victim may become victor. A test is turned into a testimony. Christian history and Christian experience amply illustrate this.

A man in India said to me, "Since I have become a Christian, I have had no more trouble." But the early Christians were in constant trouble and were very happy in spite of this.

During the Chinese-Japanese War, a Chinese church became noted for its exemption from the bombings. So many crowded into the church, they had to build a larger one. But after they dedicated it, a bomb destroyed it. This destroyed the faith of many of those who joined it because of that exemption.

Suppose it could be proved that only the righteous were exempt from sickness and trouble. What would happen to the universe? It would soon become chaotic and undependable. If a good man leaned too far over a parapet of a tall building, the law of gravity would be suspended. But if a bad man leaned over, he would fall. In the real universe the law of gravity isn't going to ask if he is good, bad, or indifferent. It will pull him down. It is a hard school, but we must know the rules.

A professor in Chicago was run over by a truck. After weeks in the hospital, he came back to the university chapel and said, "I no longer believe in a personal God. If there had been one, he would have whispered to me about that danger, but he didn't. When my leg was broken, my faith was broken." He felt that only the righteous can escape being run over by trucks. But what would happen to the character of the righteous if that were true? They would become the champion jaywalkers of the world, roaming around meditating and vegetating in the midst of the traffic. That quickness of decision which comes from a world of chance and circumstance would be taken away. I know when I cross a street that if I don't belong to the quick, I'll soon belong to the dead!

A man said to me as I was about to cross the street against the lights, "Sir, if you want to live long, walk with the lights." I have never forgotten the advice. It was good. Nor does the New Testament teach us that if you are righteous, you will be exempt from suffering. Sometimes the righteous are in trouble because they are righteous. Society demands conformity. If you fall below its standards, it will punish you. If you rise above its standards, it will persecute you. Jesus said, "Beware when all men think well of you."

Was Paul exempt? Was Jesus, the best man that ever lived, exempt? Five classes of people stood around the Cross and said: "Let God take him down and then we'll believe in him." But God didn't take him down. His head dropped upon his pulseless bosom and he died. Then where is the answer? The answer is in that very Cross. Jesus took the worst thing that could happen to him, namely, the Cross, and turned it into the healing of sin. The Cross was hate, and Jesus turned it into a revelation of love. Jesus took every-

The Divine Yes

thing that spoke against the love of God and, through it, showed the love of God. It is a Yes, a Yes over the very worst. Yes, about the nature of God. Yes, Yes, Yes!

I remember when light flashed on my mind as I was puzzled about this matter. I came across this passage and it became light: "And you will be dragged before governors and kings for my sake to bear testimony before them" (Matt. 10:18). "Oh," I said, "That is the answer. Don't expect to run away or be exempt, but use it for a testimony to Jesus." This puts us on the offensive. A Christian doesn't expect to be exempt. He expects to take things as they come, good, bad, and indifferent, and use them for a witness to Jesus. That puts a positive Yes upon every No that comes to a Christian. Everything furthers those who follow Christ. Just as an airplane goes up against resistance, against the wind, so the Christian rises on the wings of resistance. He knows how to use everything that comes, if not on account of, then in spite of.

Once I watched an eagle in the Himalayan mountains face a storm. It was a heavy storm brewing at the edge of the valley. I wondered what the eagle would do as the storm rushed through that narrow valley. Would it fly above the fury of the storm? Would it be dashed to pieces on the rocks below? No! It set its wings in such a way that the air currents sent him above the storm by their very fury. He didn't bear the storm; he used it to reach greater heights. We must learn that lesson of turning all resistance into opportunity, turning all resistance into release. Then you know how to live. It was a set of wings with the eagle that made the difference. This is a victorious way to live.

A Japanese Buddhist professor was stricken with blndness, a detached retina, at the height of his career. He couldn't believe it. He turned to the Christian faith for an answer. He came across the story of the man who was blind from birth. Jesus' answer to the question of whose sin caused the man to be born blind was, "It was not that this man sinned, or his parents, but that the works of God might be made manifest in him" (John 9:3). "Well," said the professor, "could the works of God be made manifest in my blindness?" Why not? He surrendered himself to Christ and became an evangelist. People flocked to hear the man who could take the severe blow that life had dealt him and turn it into victory. He was a happy, victorious blind man. He went to Scotland to get a higher academic degree and came back and taught theology and wrote great books the remainder of his days. He didn't ask why; he only asked how! The way of "how" turned out to be the way the universe works—making something out of it and having victory.

A man lost his eye and had to have a glass eye. He said to the doctor who was putting it in, "If you have to give me a glass eye, please put a twinkle in it!" That was victory.

One of the happiest and most useful women I have ever seen was a bedridden invalid. She had been there for forty-two years. The bedpost upon which I leaned to talk to her was worn down by people leaning upon it telling that woman all their troubles and toils and getting victory. She laughingly said to me, "I have three diseases, any one of which would have killed a

101

normal person. But they got to fighting each other inside me and forgot all about me, and I lived on." Her room was the confessional of the city. One man said, "That woman is worth more to the city than any seven clergymen." And it was true. While she was bedridden, she could use her arms to make butterfly pendants. She set up a gift shop and people bought gifts from her. When she sent in her first income tax check, she sent it with her love. When you can pay your income tax with love, that is victory! When her companion wrote to me to tell me she had died, she simply said, "Mother Bea walked into the sunset today." A beautiful phrase! But I rather think that she walked into the sunrise. Jesus was the rising morning star, not the evening star. He brings sunrises, not sunsets. He does! He is the Divine Yes. When life says No, Jesus says Yes, and this saintly woman said Yes to his Yes. They walked together into the sunrise.

Amy Carmichael was a saint in India. She established a home for three hundred girls mostly rescued from temple prostitution. Through the love and spirit of Miss Carmichael and the Spirit of God there was great joy in that home. Dr. Oscar Buck, visiting Dohnavur, South India, said to me as we walked out of the building, "The Kingdom of Heaven is like unto Dohnavur!" And it was. Miss Carmichael had been years upon her bed with acute arthritis. She said of herself, "I'm in Nero's prison, but I'm not Nero's prisoner." Most of her greatest books came out of the period when she was an invalid. She sang, when there wasn't anything to sing about—"in spite of"! She had the greatest serving Christian institution in South India. It came out of suffering into redemptive service.

Perulia Leprosarium was set up by German missionaries whose child caught leprosy in India and died there of the dread disease. Instead of saying, "Why did this happen to us?" they said. "Well, since our child has been taken by leprosy, we will establish a leprosarium for others afflicted with leprosy." Tens of thousands of patients have gone through that leprosarium because the missionaries took calamity and turned it into opportunity. Jesus was the Divine Yes that made a No into a redemptive Yes.

There is a Lee Memorial Home in Calcutta, India. The Lees had six children in school in Darjeeling, a hill station in India. One night during the monsoon rains the whole mountainside, upon which their home was built, slipped and buried all six children at once! Instead of the Lees saying, "Why did that happen to us when we were serving God in Calcutta?" they said, "Well, since our home has been broken up, we will just set up a larger home for the waif children from the streets of Calcutta." For over seventy years that home has been filled with an average of about five hundred homeless children a year. The family of six now became a family of thousands. On the monument set up to commemorate the memory of these children, there are these words: "Thanks be unto God who giveth us the victory through our Lord Jesus Christ." They went through the calamity, not somehow, but triumphantly. I heard Mrs. Lee once say, "I have never suffered anything for Christ. It has all been joy!"

A visitor visiting a mission station where a nurse was attending the sores of a person with leprosy pulled back with horror and said, "I wouldn't do that for a million dollars!" The nurse replied, smiling, "Neither would I! But I would do it for Jesus for nothing!" That was the secret of the Divine Yes.

QUESTIONS ANSWERED
FROM A CROSS

We have raised a dozen basic questions which demand an affirmative answer. And they all have an affirmative answer in Jesus Christ, the Divine Yes. Nevertheless, in no case are these easy answers. They are answers from the Cross which an English poet called Jesus' "professorial chair." Let us explore at great depth the **cruciality** of his answers to life's deepest queries.

What are some of the other questions that he raised in his tortured body as he twisted against the skyline into a question mark? Jesus' Yes is not a cheap Yes—a Pollyanna type. The questions he raises are ones that go to the heart of things. First, how far can force go in a world of this kind? As long as people believe that the last word in human affairs goes to force, force can go a long way. It can crucify the Creator of the universe on a cross. That is a very long way. It can do that today and tomorrow, but the third day—no! For Goodness rises from the dead and goodness is the last word. The guards were like dead men, and Jesus was alive. Force can go a long way, but it can only go two days. The third day God raised him from the dead. He himself is the answer, and illustrates that answer in his own body.

Second, how far can lies go? Lies can put the purest and gentlest and most truthful person on the Cross today and tomorrow, but the third day—no! The universe is not built for the success of a lie. The Tamils of South India say, "The length of the best concocted lie is just eight days." In eight days it goes to pieces upon the moral universe. When diminutive Joseph Goebbels was propaganda leader of the Nazis, the Germans had a saying, "Lies have short legs." Lies may seem good in the short run, but they are bad in the long run.

Life cannot stand upon the insecurity of a lie. A lie has nothing behind it except itself. The universe makes a lie break itself upon the universe. The universe is not broken for it is established on God's truth. So how far can lies go? A long way. They twisted his words and made them into lies. He was crucified on lies. So lies can go the first day and the second day, but the third day— no!

How many lies did it take to try to break the truth of the Gospel? They gave some persons money in those days to say that the disciples had stolen the body of Jesus. Jesus raised the question on the cross and answered it in the resurrection. How much money do you think it will take to stop the Christian Gospel now?

Third: How far can evil go in a world of this kind? Does the moral universe bend to evil? The answer is

No! Today, tomorrow, but the third day—No! The third day, evil breaks itself upon the facts of life. The word evil in English is the word live spelled backward. In other words, the universe is not built to accept evil. Only truth has the moral universe behind it. There is nothing behind evil except evil. Today and tomorrow evil may be strong, but the third day evil breaks itself upon the nature of reality. For the Christian Gospel and reality are one—in fullest accord. The sum total of reality is behind the Christian Gospel. So the Christian code which is now a character becomes a question mark today, tomorrow, but the third day it becomes an exclamation point. Jesus is alive! He is risen! And that code living in that character is alive in him.

In the play, The Terrible Meek, one of the soldiers at the crucifixion of Jesus speaks to Mary, the mother:

I tell you, woman, this dead son of yours, disfigured, shamed, spat upon, has built a kingdom this day that can never die. The living glory of him rules it. The earth is his and he made it. He and his brothers have been moulding and making it through the long ages. They are the only ones who ever really did possess it; not the proud, not the idle, not the wealthy, not the vaunting empires of the world. Something has happened up here on this hill today to shake all our kingdoms of blood and fear to the dust. The earth is his, the earth is theirs, and they made it. The meek, the terrible meek, the fierce agonizing meek, are about to enter into their inheritance.[1]

[1] Charles Rann Kennedy, The Terrible Meek (New York: Samuel French, 1912), p. 39.

People cried for his blood, at the scene of the crucifixion, but went away smiting their breasts knowing this was a place of repentance, not of rejoicing. The smiters had smitten themselves and the people and laid themselves in the tomb as they laid the Son of God in the tomb. He arose. They did not! They are buried in oblivion. He goes marching on. So the Yes he gives is a realistic Yes. It takes the worst and turns it into the best.

It should not be surprising that we find this crucial dynamic operative as a law of life. I once sat in a bus in the foothills of the Himalayas with a young English doctor who was on her way to take the place of Mary Reed. Mary Reed, a missionary, had spent a lifetime among the lepers in a mountainous region of North India and had contracted the disease herself and had never returned to her native America. She was loved, respected, and revered by the people in general. But a faithless servant, who got control of her in the last helpless days, played the Judas. When she was unconscious, he sold the bed on which she lay dying and put her on a cot. He kept the proceeds. She died on a bed not her own, helpless in the face of cheating in her own household. I asked the doctor if she knew about this story. She said she did. I then asked if she were still going on and she replied, "I do it for him!" The doing it for him made the difference.

A Canadian missionary had to destroy the contaminated house of a person with leprosy, and then he went on furlough. On board ship he developed a strange disease, and when they stopped in London, it was diagnosed as leprosy. He went on to Canada to a hut made of logs out in the wilderness. He stayed there alone with Jesus. A friend from India came to see him. In talking about the old days in India together, the friend showed that he felt sorry for the missionary with leprosy. So the man with leprosy said, "Wait a minute. I feel that you pity me and feel sorry for me. Don't! These logs that make up my cabin are glorious with the love of Christ. I am not alone! He and I are living it out together. This is no place for sympathy for it is a privilege!"

"Without him, not one step over the threshold; but with him, anywhere!" The open hand of Jesus as I clasp it is the greatest security I know in the universe. I take it with humility and gratitude for the privilege.

Some of the outcastes of southern India became Christians. Some of the higher caste Hindus wanted to punish them and burned the fields of one of these Christians. As he went out to put out the blaze, they caught him and cut off his hands. This Christian had been taught by the YMCA secretary. However, the YMCA secretary was deeply incensed at what had happened and wanted to prosecute the culprits. He said: "Let's take up a collection for prosecuting the people who did it. We have their names." They took up a collection and sent it to this Christian, now handless.

The handless Christian said to the YMCA secretary, "Sahib, you taught me the Christian Gospel and the Christian Gospel teaches us to love our enemies and to pray for those who despitefully use you and persecute you. Now you are telling me something else. You are telling me to prosecute. How can I? You introduced me to Christ, and he teaches me to forgive. I am sorry, I can't take the money." The handless Christian took the hand of Jesus and walked into the future with his head up and his heart up in victory. I can never forget him.

One last illustration—and literally, a last offering—is the most impressive. A Christian woman, a woman of prayer who was an invalid, lay on her bed and wrote letters to prisoners in various prisons in Japan. Someone suggested that she write to a man who was a famous prisoner being tried for murder. She wrote one of her wonderful letters to him. It went deep into the soul of the prisoner, and he became a Christian. He wrote to her and told her that he was going to pray, now that he was a Christian, for Jesus to heal her. And he did heal her.

The prisoner became famous for his Christianity. Many of the other prisoners became Christians because of him. Then came the day for his execution. The pastor in Nagoya, Japan told me the story. He and the prisoner had communion at the base of the scaffold, and the condemned man talked to the officials that were gathered there. He said to them, "The church has baked me a cake for my last meal as my last request. It is good and I wish I could give you some. You are doing your duty. You are not executing the man who did the deed, for he is already dead. He is risen in this new man that stands before you and is willing to take the penalty for the dead man and be buried with Christ. But I am not the same man."

He was the only serene and quiet man there. The rest were shaken. When he got to the top of the scaffold, they wanted to put a black cap over his head, but he refused it. He said, "I am not afraid for I will be with my Savior and Lord." When the trapdoor was sprung, the last thing the people could hear as he fell was a strain of "Nearer My God to Thee."

There was a Divine Yes in the midst of a human No. They said he couldn't live. The Divine Yes said he does live. The Divine Yes sounded amidst the human No.

In all these cases the Divine Yes replaced the human No. It was the power of the Cross, sacrificial love. The cross of Jesus is not a negation, but an affirmation. The final power is alive today and keeping the world alive. Jesus is Lord! He answers Yes to life and to the world—and he gives this final answer from a Cross!

HEALING:
UNCONDITIONAL AND
CONDITIONAL

As I have already said, I have written all my books out of the necessity to meet some need. The need produced a certain pressure and the pressure produced the book, perhaps after long thought. This book and the chronology came together as if they were Siamese twins.

Let me once again touch on what happened. I have referred to it briefly in the beginning, but now months have gone by. This stroke came without any warning and without apparent previous cause. I was not overly tired. As I have said, I had gone through a two-month evangelistic crusade in Japan without any strain or appreciable drain. I found that at eighty-seven God was using me as effectively, perhaps even more effectively, than he had as a younger person. In Japan I discovered that my age was an asset, instead of a liability, in working with young people, for the Japanese respect age and maturity. A large part of my audiences were young people. I had a sense of knowing I was doing the will of God by the power of God. Then suddenly I was thrown back on the resources of God as never before. The stroke hit me! Naturally I began to wonder whether or not I should be healed.

In years past I have experienced unconditional healing. There is a tablet at the back of a church in Lucknow, India, which reads: "Near this spot Stanley Jones knelt a physically broken man and arose a physically well man." The story back of the tablet was this: After eight and a half years in India, I had had a ruptured appendix and as a result tetanus set in. This caused me to have a nervous collaspe when everything would leave me in a state of confusion. I thought I would have to give up the mission field and the ministry to try to regain my shattered health.

I was in this church in Lucknow, kneeling at the back alone when God said to me, "Are you yourself ready for the work to which I have called you?" My answer was, "No, Lord, I am done for. I have reached the end of my resources and I cannot go on." His reply, "If you will turn that over to me and not worry about it, I'll take care of it." I replied, "Lord, I close the bargain right here." I arose from my knees knowing I was a well man.

My feet scarcely touched the earth as I walked home that night. I wondered if I should tell this. I felt I should and did. I was committed. For over half a century after that I have been speaking from two to five times a day, taking no vacations except to write a book. I became strongest where I was weakest, namely in nervous energy.

I have also experienced conditional healing. When, twenty years ago, the doctor discovered sugar in my blood and that I was diabetic, my Inner Voice said to me, "In me you are well and whole. You go on with your evangelistic touring to Japan and elsewhere, and there will be a minimum of strain with a maximum of result." And so it happened. But this time it was conditional for I had to adopt the discipline of leaving nearly all sugar out of my diet. As I did that, I was well and whole. But if I didn't do it, I wasn't well and I wasn't whole. This I call conditional healing.

The question with me regarding this stroke is whether or not God will give me conditional healing immediately or unconditional and absolute healing. I am open to whatever healing he sends, conditional or unconditional, for I believe in both and I am open to him. If I have to live as a physically limited man the balance of my days, I can accept that. Or I can accept his complete and total healing. Whatever he sends, I will accept it with his grace to use it to glorify him. I give it back to him to settle which it will be.

But now I must insist that I am open to total healing. When I have sufficiently been made into his image and especially into his image of receptivity, I expect to receive his fullness of grace so that his health becomes mine, his victory becomes mine. Not because I'm good or worthy, but because I belong to eternal goodness and worthiness in him. Grace will be written over the healing, and over the consequent health there will be no room for boasting. When we talk about healing, we talk about the gracious gift to God, but there is no room for boasting.

I once went into the garden of Gethsemane to spend the night there and feel with Jesus the agony of those hours. I took a blanket, a hand lantern, and my Bible. About midnight it occurred to me to read the account again. When I came to the end of the account, the full impact of its meaning burst upon me. I nearly jumped from my seat. For the end was not in the bloody drops of sweat and the sorrow that weighed him to the ground. The end was in his words, "Arise, let us be going." He had decided to face it head on! The direction, even though it meant death, was his choosing.

If Jesus had been miraculously delivered from the mob who came to destroy him, to show that God was with him, it would be easy to believe in him, but it would mean that Jesus was aloof and apart from the suffering that man knows. But God chose another way to show his power. Jesus didn't ask for a miracle of deliverance. He asked for the strength to drink the cup and endure the cross that he might pay the price of man's redemption. The cross is not a monument of deliverance, but a perpetual symbol of how God overcame hate by love, evil with good, and death by eternal life. Jesus was not asking for a miracle of deliverance to be perfomed before that crowd. He was accepting the cross as a way of life. It would not be a miracle if he had been saved apart from the cross, but it was a miracle of saving men through the cross. It was a miracle of obedience and self-surrender.

Now that question has come to me in a smaller but very personal way. Should I ask to be delivered from this whole stroke and its effect, or should I take it as a limitation which has come to me that I might glorify him and show a workable way to live to others—to be thrown back on grace, so as to stay within the category of those who have to win through suffering? Will I take the limit of deliverance or bear the marks of the Lord Jesus in my own body? I am faced with this complexity because I am a part of the world's calamities and suffering, as well as partaker of grace.

Now I believe that it was this question that Jesus faced when the Greeks came. I don't think they came for an interview, but for a decision. They saw that Jesus, if he went on the way he was going, would end on the cross. As I have said, I believe they came to ask him, not to go to Jerusalem, but to go to Athens as a teacher of philosophy, put his Gospel into Greek thought, spread it through the world, and thus spread his Kingdom. If he went to Jerusalem, it meant a cross; if he went to Athens it would mean he would live long, honored, and respected as a great teacher and philosopher. He went to Jerusalem, took the Cross, and redeemed a world.

Could I, in a lesser way, face this cross and help redeem a world in however small a way? Could I, even I, add my small yes of response to the Divine Yes which stands behind the whole universe?

USING OUR SUFFERING

Once I saw a beautiful church made up of rejected pieces of marble that were brought together into a whole. It made a very beautiful sanctuary. I have picked out certain things, pieces left over from the wreckage of my life, and am trying to put them together into a temple of God—a workable way to live. If your life has gone to pieces, take the pieces and give them back to God, and he will make something out of them. It is amazing what God can do with a broken heart, or life, when you give him all the pieces.

So I am collecting the pieces of the wreckage that came with the stroke and am trying to put them together into a living whole. I have been called upon to illustrate my own teaching, and I find it is easier to preach on how to use defeat and calamity than to illustrate it, which I am now called upon to do! This is exciting also for not many people have a second chance to tie up the meaning of their writing by illustrating it in their own lives. But I have that chance. I look on it as an opportunity and not as a catastrophe. I am trying to put the pieces of my life together or turn them over to God to make something out of them.

So instead of coasting into a landing at eighty-eight, I have an opportunity to illustrate the meaning of what I have been talking about for more than seventy years. It is difficult, but very important and necessary. God gives me this opportunity. This book is the turning over of the pieces of my life in order to put them together again in relaxed symmetry and cohesion. Nevertheless, it is an attempt to put the pieces together on a higher level, and to not only write a book, but to illustrate it. Better than to preach a sermon is to be one!

Years ago some friends of mine in the restaurant business in Oklahoma City were leaving to go further west to begin over again, for they had not made a success of their business there. The wife had prepared a chicken basket dinner for them to eat as they drove along. She was just getting ready to hand him a piece of chicken, when the car hit a bump in the road and the chicken fell on the floor. She picked it up and said, "I'm sorry, dear, but I'm afraid I'm serving you 'Chicken-in-the rough.'" He said, "Wait a minute! We are going back!" They turned the car around and went back and founded a business which they called "Chicken-in-the-Rough," and made a fortune. They took a bump in the road and let it bump them into a million-dollar idea. He dedicated that fortune and himself to God.

This stroke has been a bump toward the end of the road of my life, but instead of it just being "Chicken-in-the-Rough," it is going to be an illustration of the meaning of not merely bearing opposition and sorrow, but using them and making something out of them. This has been my message all my life, and now it will have to be the message through my life. By his grace I think I can do it.

It was said of the Samaritans that they would not let Jesus come into their village because his face was set as if he were going to Jerusalem, so they refused him entrance. James and John wanted to call down fire from heaven, but Jesus refused them and went to another village. Is that the open door? If life shuts you out of one village, does life also have another village to which you can go? Yes, I have found that when life shuts one door, it opens another if you have eyes to see and initiative to follow.

As a violinist tightens the strings of the violin, he does not do it to torture them, but to bring out music better than before. This pause in my life work is not misery; it is music in the making. It was said that the early Christians overcame that pagan world of wrong for they out-thought the pagans, outlived the pagans, out-suffered the pagans, out-died the pagans. That is what we must do in a world of this kind.

The Finns have a word that has become a very national word—sisu—meaning "a little more." They can take a little more, suffering a little more than others. By enduring a little more than others, they have grown more. Therefore, they are very wonderful people, some of the greatest in the world. Many great Christians, many great movements, have been produced by being able to use the word sisu—by going a little further in their moral and spiritual daring, by suffering a little more. The Christian word is "in." In him the Divine Yes is sounded. It is not through him or by him but in him.

A missionary in China was being led to her execution. In the midst of it as they walked along, she got to thinking how very funny it would be to look back and see her head rolling down the hill as her spirit was going off to Glory. She began to laugh. Her captor said to her, "What are you laughing about?" She told them. They stopped and said to her, "Well, if it is going to make you so happy, then we aren't going to do it." So she laughed herself out of her own execution!

Take the Madagascar Christians, when they were being hunted by their enemies because they were Christians. They were in a cave and wanted to sing. Their leader said, "Don't sing as it will reveal our hiding place, and we will be murdered." They said, "We have to sing. But we will sing in our minds." They were discovered, however, and they sang while being hurled over a cliff. It was resounding, not a quiet whisper. It was something that had to be shouted even while being hurled to death over a cliff.

I spoke in a cathedral in Salisbury, the capital of Rhodesia, and I quoted what had happened in a mission school in Rhodesia where thirty young people went up to take the Cambridge examination which was in English, a foreign language for the Africans. One hundred percent passed, some with honors. The one at the top of the thirty was a girl in the very place where earlier a girl had presented herself to go to school and caused a riot, for girls were not supposed to be educated. This was change in one decade. She had won top honors. I said to the white congregation in the cathedral, "That examination result is the doom of your new constitution based on the inferiority of the black and the superiority of the white." One white man, who was the Supreme Court judge, resigned as he could not enforce such a constitution and he predicted that the explosion would come within three to five years. It came in three. He read, in the light of the burning buildings, in the constitution of the universe, "Thou shalt love thy neighbor as thyself."

The sign in the Christian faith is: "Ye shall find a babe." It was a person. The Muslims of India said that the name of Mohammed was written in the sky, in the clouds. The sign was a portent, but not a person—an "It." In the Christian faith it is not an "It," it is a Him. And it is not a No, negating life and the world; but a Yes able to turn the negation of suffering into an affirmation of significance. No wonder one of the early church Fathers said that Jesus turns our sunsets into sunrises!

A DIARY OF VICTORY
IN AFFLICTION

Introductory Note: These reflections were recorded over a period of about a year. After his stroke Dr. Jones was hospitalized in the Baptist Memorial Hospital, Oklahoma City. After two weeks he was transferred to Boston where for a fortnight he was in the Massachusetts General Hospital. Following that he spent some weeks in a nearby private institution, Massachusetts Rehabilitation Hospital. This was followed by a stay at the Holy Ghost Hospital (now Youville) in Cambridge, Massachusetts, where much skilled and loving care was shown him by the doctors and the Roman Catholic sisters. In May, 1972, he returned to India to Sat Tal Ashram in the Himalayas, a place he greatly loved. On this venturesome journey he was accompanied by his son-in-law, Bishop James K. Mathews, and two of his three grandchildren, Anne and Stanley. The flight was interrupted for a rest period of twenty-four hours in Frankfurt, where the German Methodist sisters saw to his every comfort and sent him refreshed on his way. In July he was strong enough to go to a World Ashram Congress in Jerusalem. Following his return to India the same month, he went again to Sat Tal and finally to Clara Swain Hospital in Bareilly, where he died January 25, 1973.

———————◆———————

The amazing thing to me was that with the stroke in no uncertain terms came the attitude I had to take. I was to go through this, not just somehow, but triumphantly and victoriously!—December, 1971, Boston

———————◆———————

I have received thousands of letters since my stroke. One received from a very devoted Christian said, "Dear Friend, I have been greatly disappointed and discouraged that God's child like you, who has given all his life to serve his Redeemer, our Lord Jesus Christ, should get such a paralytic attack." He felt that if you were only righteous, you would be exempt from things that others have to meet. This man represents many. It is the problem of Job all over again.— January, 1972, Boston

———————◆———————

In this rehabilitation center where I am they have all the techniques of prolonging life. I am grateful that

123

the stroke struck me at eighty-eight. I said to myself, "Outwardly you have lived as long as most people. Physically I may be going downhill, but I've found a landing. It seems to me that many people here in this institution have no purpose in being here except to prolong their lives, and I can't see how merely prolonging life does anything for them or for humanity.

I am grateful I have had so many years in the world of Life—with a capital L. Now if I have to be cut off from some of that world of Life, I want it to be in a quality of being, as a proof that the Christian way works. I want the quality of being to be the goal of my life instead of the prolonging of years. When I am no longer "alive" on the inside, then I do not see why I should be kept alive on the outside. Once the Holy Spirit said to me, "I'll keep you alive as long as you are 'alive.'" I am grateful, for when I am no longer "alive within" I do not want to be kept alive on the outside.
—January, 1972, Boston

I realize more and more in this rehabilitation center, which is second to none, that there is an attempt to find joy in the secular manner through secular methods. But I see no signs of joy in the people assembled here for rehabilitation. Their faces are dead faces. The joy of the Cross is joy in spite of, not on account of.

When the stroke destroyed the muscles that we smile with, it meant that I couldn't smile any more for I didn't have the apparatus. Now I am in the process of creating that apparatus to express the deep down joy of the promise that I shall have both the muscles and the message required. I smile the smile of inner laughter.—**February, 1972, Boston**

———————◆———————

One of the nurses said, as she was trying to teach me to walk, "You have the most contagious laughter I have ever heard." Contagious laughter? It was the first time it was ever said to me, but it could be said of me now. I laugh and the world laughs with me. I have cosmic backing for my laughter. "He who laughs last, laughs best." I am having this with laughter at the closing of my life. It seems to be the best of all because it ties everything up into the statement QED "which was to be demonstrated." This has to be proved and is proving itself.

Paul stood before the Roman court and said to King Agrippa, "I would to God that not only you but also all who hear me this day might become such as I am" (Acts 26:29). Then he added a courteous gesture, "except for these chains." Apart from these chains, I wish everyone had what I have. The interesting thing was no one laughed when Paul said this. And nobody ever since has laughed—because it was sober fact. The prisoner had something which those who had captured him did not have. Paul was telling them he wanted all of them to have what he had, except chains.

I can say to the world, "I want everybody to have what I have, except for this stroke." The stroke so far has been a stroke to let the Glory out. I have spent these months looking into the face of Jesus with an unobstructed gaze and what I see is wonderful. It is redemptive, satisfying, and exciting. "That one dear face, far from vanishing, rather grows; becomes my universe that feels and knows." I'll have the opportunity before I go of finding the demonstration and I have found it. I would end up by saying it has been proved and is proving itself. I am not trying to prove it. It is self-verifying.—February, 1972, Boston

"When you were young, you girded yourself and walked where you would; but when you are old, you will stretch out your hands, and another will gird you and carry you where you do not wish to go" (John 21:18). "Another" leads me where I do want to go. I want to go with him and him alone. Where he is, here is heaven. Where he is not, there is hell. So it is very simple. I can go anywhere he is and that will be heaven enough for me. I have found it so and believe I shall find it so until the end.

If Peter stumbled along the way, the last few steps of the way he took firmly and with decisiveness. Tradition says that when Peter was about to be crucified, he said, "Don't crucify me with my head up, but down, for I am not worthy to be crucified like my Lord."

If this tradition is true, it gives a final word about Peter. He could have said, No, and said it with curses, but he finally said Yes and said it with humility. So Jesus didn't fail with Peter, and Peter didn't fail Jesus. It was a Divine Yes with the most resounding emphasis that could be made. At the end he said Yes to a will that was his freedom. He has strengthened the world, for his last attitude was the most important one. —February, 1972, Boston

---

Another therapist when giving me lessons in walking this week said, "You are giving me back my faith again." A nurse said yesterday, "What is happening here is creating a sensation in you." Joy, when there is nothing to be joyful about except the fact of belonging to a joyous Kingdom which cannot be shaken and to a person who does not change. Another nurse exclaimed that it was sheer wonderment that I wasn't enduring my stroke, but using it! It is a Yes, a Divine Yes, to a Kingdom that when everything outer is being shattered, everything within me remains unshattered and intact! It works to the degree that you work it! —March, 1972, Boston

---

My doctor in this rehabilitation center told me I could go anywhere I wanted to go and do anything I wanted to do, even to the extent of going to India. He said I was a very strong man. But my strength is not in me, but in him, who when he calls me to do a thing also gives the power to do that thing. It is not my ability, but my response to his ability. It isn't what happens to us that matters, but what we do with what happens to us that counts. The verse that my life has turned on is, "You will be [brought] before governors

127

and kings for my sake to bear testimony before them.
. . . Do not be anxious how you are to speak or what
you are to say; for what you are to say will be given to
you in that hour" (Matt. 10:18-19). We can turn everything into a testimony. The opposition can become
open doors. Everything furthers those who follow
Christ.—March, 1972, Boston

I am free to demonstrate the kind of life I have been
advocating. I am free to demonstrate the unshakable
Kingdom and the unchanging Person. I am free for I
am in bondage to both!—March, 1972, Boston

———————◆———————

I am thankful that even as a boy I came to terms
with the race problem. The problem is not race, for
clearly a variety of races is the will of God. It is a
problem of attitude of those who practice racial preju-
dice. This is sin. Long ago I saluted a rising race—the
Negroes.

I have gone on my way, which is his way, and I am
now dictating this in a Roman Catholic institution in
Cambridge, near Boston. It is supposed to be one of
the best in the country for rehabilitation of strokes. In-
terestingly enough, while it is a Roman Catholic institution, it is run by a Negro Protestant doctor as head.
This is a sign of how far even our sick society has
moved and I am grateful.

I thank God I have lived long enough to see giant
strides in the resolving and healing of this disease of
racism in our society. I could wish that I would see it
entirely wiped out, not only in our own nation but

throughout the lands of earth. But, perhaps, that would be the Kingdom of God fully come!—April, 1972, Cambridge.

There is a crucifix on the wall of my room. As an evangelical evangelist, I am not supposed to believe much in crucifixes. I would rather believe in the Cross. One of my best friends, a medical doctor, was converted looking at a crucifix in a Roman Catholic hospital. He was called to see a "river rat," a drunkard who lived near the river. The patient was bleeding from a stomach ulcer. The doctor looked at him and said, "What you need is Jesus Christ," then turned and left him. The man reacted in great anger, but he also became a Christian. He later became a pastor in the very "river rat" section of town from which he had been snatched.

The doctor himself was not then a Christian. Later, he, himself, was in a hospital suffering from a stomach ulcer. In desperation he fixed his attention on the crucifix hanging in his room and was soundly converted. He became the head of our Ashram in the state of Tennessee. He has a radio program that he uses to tell people how to find Christ. He went to Palestine and while he was being shown the Garden Tomb, he witnessed so powerfully to the guide that he led the man to Christ. The doctor did a very unethical thing, medically speaking, to tell his patient that he needed Christ and then walk away doing nothing more. But unwittingly he did the very thing the man needed.—April, 1972, Cambridge

———————◆———————

Everyone comes from his peak to a gradual or sudden fall into old age. A very lovely woman said to me during my illness, "I hate to grow old, but I feel it gradually coming upon me." She was going into a gradual decline, a slow aging. She didn't like the process for she could feel the creeping paralysis of old age. There is a way to come into old age with a crash. Apparently I have come into it in that way. I have been prepared for it by a long series of falls which left me more or less intact through the years.

———————◆———————

Along the way I have learned the art of falling well. I was walking rather briskly up a steep incline to the chapel of Sat Tal Ashram for morning prayers a few years ago. I was somewhat late so I was in haste. I stubbed my toe on a stone protruding out of the pathway. As a result I took a dive straight forward, like a dive into second base in baseball, on the gravel pathway. I picked myself up and searched for hurts and bruises, but didn't find any. I said to myself, "All is well." I went on to the group, but a little later I had a severe internal hemorrhage. I was puzzled for there was no pain involved. I took it in my stride for my inner voice kept saying, "It will pass." I told my daughter about it, and when I returned to America, she insisted I have a checkup at the Lahey Clinic in Boston to see if there might be a tumor. After a thorough examination the doctors found nothing. Everything was clear. I had fallen well. Usually I have managed to fall forward!

My most serious fall, at about eighty-five years of age, was also at Sat Tal Ashram in India. Our estate has two sections, divided by two government lakes with a channel connecting the two. There was a large log across the channel. Coming back from a dinner party, I decided to save myself walking three-quarters of a mile by crossing the log. It was a peeled log of pine and very slippery. Some of the young people helped me by holding my hand, but I slipped about halfway across and fell eleven feet down into the channel. I picked myself up to see if I was hurt, but I was only shaken up a bit with no damage. I didn't wish to be conquered by a log, so I climbed up and straddled it and inched my way across to the other side and felt triumphant! Each fall left nothing but a shakeup. I felt I was being prepared for something, but little did I know what it would be.

When I came to the fall—the autumn—of my life, to this stroke which left me in shambles, I knew that the only Christian way to fall was to fall on my knees and thank God that though outwardly I am only a half person, in him I am whole and well and the same person as before. If I had to choose between the two alternatives of being a half person inwardly and whole outwardly, or a half person outwardly and a whole person inwardly, I would gladly choose the latter. I had fallen, but I had fallen into the arms of Grace.
—April, 1972, Cambridge

Recently I had a visitor from England. He had come over to talk to the American World Council leaders about the world spiritual awakening. He said, "I see a great necessity for it, but I am somewhat pessimistic and afraid it will all end in talk." I said, "No, I don't think so, for this time there is a world movement behind a spiritual awakening for the world—a world pressure. Society is going to pieces at the seams and won't turn unless we have some kind of spiritual awakening that creates new men and women who can create a new world. It is not just merely a movement among Christians. Everybody needs it."—April, 1972, Cambridge

---

I have learned that if you are blocked on one road in life, you can always find another that will open up to you. If you can't go here, you can go there. We don't have to be afraid for if we can't do this, we can do that. They blocked Jesus by not receiving him for his face was set to go to Jerusalem. The disciples wanted to call down fire, but Jesus just went to another village. We can always go to another village. Don't bear your oppositions; use them. There may be a pause in my program, but a pause in music is music in the making. So every pause can make us tougher and more mature. We can learn to take the initiative, like the airplane that goes up against the wind, using the wind to lift it off the ground. "If life throws a dagger at you, take hold of it by the handle and cut your way through opposition." This is the secret.

In John 16:20 Jesus says, "Your sorrow will turn into joy." The outcome is the criterion. This is to say that divine pain brings forth joy. What kind of pain are you coming out to? Is it a pain divine or a pain of a strain? "Pagans waste their pain." They don't come out to anything, no divine end. But when it is divine pain, like the pain of the Cross, it is not a wasted pain, but contributive pain—like the pains of a mother in child-birth.

A pastor spoke on painted sticks. He watched a worm crawl on a green painted pole expecting to get some luscious thing at the top. But when he got to the top he just turned round and round and had to descend back again for there were no luscious leaves at the top. A millionaire in the audience came up to the pastor and said, "Have you any message for a tired millionaire? I have been climbing painted sticks all my life and find I must retrace my steps. I am very tired."

But a Christian who belongs to the unshakable Kingdom and the unchanging Person climbs poles that reach further and further into the infinite with no dis-illusionment. You keep saying to yourself, "This is for real! This is for real!" People would say to me in my present condition, "You have climbed a painted stick which in the end has let you down into collapse." Into a collapse or a contribution? It can be contributive and creative.

"Your sorrow will turn into joy." It is no cheap joy imposed, but a joy that has come out of pain. The Christian's way to joy is through a Cross, therefore it is a joy that has meaning, depth, and value. It was said of the early Christians' joy that they were continually in trouble, but continually in joy. This, then, is a joy with value in it.

I thought I knew joy, until this stroke. But now I know joy with a red streak in it. The stroke is the streak. It has turned everything into a new value. The world tries to get joy, but only gets pleasure—sometimes and briefly. The Christian gets joy out of the heart of pain.—May, 1972, Cambridge

The Vedanta philosophy of India depicts God as unrelated, without bounds. He has no relationships with any human beings. So, having no relationships, he has no trouble. But the God and Father of our Lord Jesus Christ is a related God. He is related to men in self-giving love. Whatever hits man, hits him. Therefore, his joy is the joy of sharing whatever falls upon man. A Hindu doctor, chairman of one of my meetings in India, once said, "We must not entangle God in the human relationships. If he were tangled in human relationships, he would be involved, therefore unhappy, therefore imperfect, therefore not God." They try to keep God perfect by keeping him perfectly isolated.

What is the secret of joy in this universe? Who are the happy and the unhappy? I can tell you in a sentence. The most unhappy people in the world are those who won't do anything for anybody, anywhere. They are disentangled, so they think. But instead of becoming disentangled, they become entangled in their own unhappiness.

Every self-centered person is unhappy. So if God

should be unrelated, he would be unhappy. He would be the center of a cosmic misery. But God deliberately entangles himself in the world to pass on his own joy of self-giving love as a God that knows the deepest and most wonderful joy in this world.

The happy people are those who go out to deliberately take upon themselves trouble, sorrow, and pain in behalf of others. In the midst of doing this their hearts begin to sing with joy. This is "pain divine." It brings forth joy for it is pain set to music. Someone has said the Negro Spirituals are "pain set to music." They are. Listen to this: "Nobody knows the trouble I've seen. Nobody knows, but Jesus. . . . Glory Hallelujah!" People who can begin and end like this have something to give to the world. It begins with depths (trouble), and goes to the heights (Glory Hallelujah!). We can sing when there is nothing to sing about except that we must sing as we have something to sing about.
—May, 1972, Cambridge

———◆———

I have had six months of life under the stroke. I haven't read a thing in six months though kind friends have read to me. I see but in a haze. I have been able to turn over once in my bed from one side to the other, but only once in the first month. My speech is thick and sometimes muddled, but my one big joyous thing is that the stroke did not touch the right side of my brain. The first thing that they announced to me on coming out of the initial shock was that the brain cells which preside over morality and intelligence were intact. I see that life is good. Evil has invaded it and suffering has invaded it, but life, as life, is good!

Jesus came that I might have life and have it more abundantly. He is not only life, but he is life with a Yes in it, a Divine Yes. The universe and everything in it says that life is good. Evil has invaded it, but evil is an intrusion. Evil is an attempt to live life without the Divine Plan. It can't be done. It turns out badly and sadly every time it is tried. What is bad is bad for us, and what is good is good for us. But life is good, and Jesus has come that we might have life and have it more abundantly.

The answer to the problems of life is not less life but more life. I'm finding by experiment and demonstration that one can have more life within himself. If I keep my eyes on Jesus, I can say to life, "Come on, I'm healed at the heart. Let life do its worst or its best. I'll take it and make it into something else by his grace and power." So the demonstration is "demonstrating."—May, 1972, Cambridge

———◆———

With the help of my son-in-law, my granddaughter, and grandson I have returned to the ashram at Sat Tal in these beloved Himalaya mountains in North India. My grandchildren are caring for me until others can take their place when they return home. Naturally, I am deeply grateful for them.

I am taking an active part in the program of the ashram. I am carried to the meetings in a **dandi**, which looks like a coffin or carriage, carried by four men. It reminds me of the paralytic in Mark 2, who was "carried by four men." I go three times a day as I take my turn as speaker in the ashram program in the chapel and at the lakeside. In between times I am learning to walk when I was told I could not walk again. I am walking with help and attending prayers, giving lectures and conducting classes, as I have done in the ashram for over half a century. Again, I was told I would never lecture or preach again, but I am doing it and my voice is improving.—June, 1972, Sat Tal

---

I am dictating this to an Indian stenographer and then my manuscript is read to me by one of the members of the Sat Tal Ashram because my eyesight has been practically nil. I have just returned from a visit to the best eye specialist in India and the verdict was: "We can do nothing for you. Our advice is to pray." So this last hope for earthly eyesight is gone. I can echo the words of General William Booth, "I have served God and the people with my eyesight and I will serve God and the people with my blindness." Two top specialists, both of them non-Christian, came to the same conclusion that nothing can be done. In the words of one of them I can "surrender to God and pray."—June, 1972, Sat Tal

---

This surrender to God is victory, and I believe the promise made to me that "you will have sufficient eyesight to carry on your work" will be fulfilled. If not, then I go on my way rejoicing. I feel it now clear. The top scientists in America said, "You will never walk,"

137

and the top scientists in India said that nothing could be done for my eyesight, except to surrender to God and pray. Science in both cases says that they are helpless beyond the wheelchair and prayer. In a way I am relieved. Everything is clear now for a miracle, or to copy the example of General Booth. I accept the situation, and I believe I will come out with the Divine Yes. I am entirely in his hands and his hands mean the Divine Yes. Now the coast is clear. I look forward with joy to the outcome. If I can take one over the other, I'll be in bondage. If I can take both, I'm free.—June, 1972, Sat Tal

———————◆———————

It is a solemn reflection to realize that here we are back where it all began. The Holy Spirit's work has become worldwide, "beginning at Jerusalem." No disciple of Jesus Christ can be here without the deepest searching of heart for here the one whom we call the Divine Yes culminated his ministry: here he taught; here he suffered; here he was crucified; here he arose gloriously from the tomb to reign forevermore in the experience of those who have said "yes" to his Yes!

The occasion is the convening of a World Ashram Congress. Of ashrams I have written briefly in this book and elsewhere. The trip from Delhi to Tel Aviv and then up to the Holy City I have stood very well. As always those who have looked after me have been kindness and consideration personified, and I am grateful. No wonder Von Hügel said that a Christian is one who cares! Usually we think of those words in the sense that we are the ones doing the caring—for others. More often than not, however, we are on the receiving end of care from others. God seems to see to that.

Frankly, I did not at first favor the holding of this World Ashram Congress. Now my attitude has changed. Ashramites have gathered here from east and west, from south and north; literally, from the ends of the earth. Their presence symbolizes the fact that the movement has matured. Some ashrams have been held in six continents and now, increasingly, the momentum is being carried within the various regions and not relying excessively on America. This is especially true in Japan, Scandinavia, and Canada as well as India. It was a moving experience for me to be able to speak a final word to these comrades of the Way with whom I have been associated through the years. The Ashram movement is now theirs—and his! It "seemed good to the Holy Spirit and to us"—as the first Christians used to put it—to commend the movement into their hands. As they link hands together and with the hands of God, none of us need fear the future. Tomorrow we return to India.—July, 1972, Jerusalem

---

Thank you, Divine Yes. I have gone through, with you, for these months now. They have been months of Communion, not with a principle for I'm not a principle, I'm a person, and I have had communion with you —the Divine Yes. You have brought me out on the Yes side of everything that has come up.

Concerning my eyesight, you have assured me that I

would get enough sight to carry on as I have been doing. Second, you have given me sufficient power of locomotion so I'll not have to stay in a completely helpless condition. Third, my voice is coming back, instead of this croaking voice I have had since the collapse. Fourth, my left hand has come back as a handmaiden, as told me in prayer. I will get aid from it, but not full aid. Then, as you have said, there are limitations, but none that will limit me as a person and limit my influence for the Kingdom. The limitations will all open the door to Divine Grace. That means that you and I will work it out together. I am to be a man of Grace.

So far I have spent many hours with you, and there hasn't been a boresome hour. I have been inwardly excited and inwardly assured that this is the Way. I haven't had a blue or discouraged hour in the months of this period of adjustment since the stroke. I accept the limitations because the limitations are opening the door for me to possess the Kingdom and let the Kingdom possess me. So far I'm satisfied and grateful. I proceed with the appointment.—July, 1972, Sat Tal

---

The Christian faith is not centered in a book, or an it. The book is the inspired revelation of him. The Bible is not the revelation of God, but the inspired record of the revelation as seen in the face of Jesus Christ. Great is the wonder of our religion. "Who does not admit how profound is the divine truth of our religion?—it is He. . . ." (I Tim. 3:16 Moffatt.) So this faith of ours is not in a group. It is in a Person. The group is composed of some people. But the Person is open to all. Therefore, the center of our faith is a Person who is open to all people, everywhere, on equal terms. So the Christian faith is relationship of a Person to a person, individually and collectively.—August, 1972, Sat Tal

———◆———

When in Luke's Gospel Jesus revealed himself to his disciples as the Messiah, the Son of God, it was a great moment. For what he was like, they must be like. He was unique in being the Son of God, but the qualities that made up "the Son of God" must be in their characters. He lost no time in telling them that he was going to lose his life in Jerusalem.—August, 1972, Sat Tal

———◆———

As I have labored and prayed toward physical recuperation, I have had plenty of time to think of ashrams. Much of the time I have been here at the Sat Tal Ashram, a spot greatly beloved in my experience.

In the late 1920s I decided I needed a group discipline, both for myself and for my work. So in 1930 I invited two others, one an Indian minister and the other a retired English missionary, to join me in establishing a Christian ashram—a place of spiritual retreat.

The term **ashram** comes from the Hindu tradition, from the Sanskrit a "from" and **shram** "hard work," a retreat from hard work into a forest school under a **guru** or teacher, where in simplicity and disciplined

141

corporate living the disciples, or chelas, would seek for moksha—salvation. Other authorities say the a in ashram is intensive, and that the word means an intensification of hard work. Far from being a cessation of hard work, it is an intensification of it, for it is hard work both to discipline one's self and to engage with others in spiritual renewal and service.

We were able to obtain a beautiful estate in the foothills of the Himalayas (5,000 feet) at Sat Tal (seven lakes). Here we started our first Christian ashram, putting Christian content into the Indian spirit—inner poise, spiritual sensitiveness, devotion, simplicity with an ascetic tinge. In this indigenous mold the Indian Christian as well as the non-Christian could be at home. We hadn't the slightest idea that we were beginning something that would become a world movement.

Some people would surmise because we have used Hindu terms that therefore the Christian Ashram is an amalgamation between Christianity and Hinduism. Nothing could be further from the reality.

The guru makes the ashram—for good or ill. The Christian ashram as a guru too, though not a human guru, for no man is wise enough or good enough to be the center of a religious movement—only divine shoulders can bear that responsibility. Jesus Christ is the guru of our Ashram. Guru in Sanskrit means "dispeller of darkness," and one could scarcely think of a more appropriate designation for Jesus Christ who is the Light of the World. The Christian ashram revolves around Jesus Christ. That is important and vital. It also means that all Christians can come together around the Person of Christ. It also means that non-

Christians can unite around Christ, while they are often reluctant to accept Christianity in the Western garments in which it is so often clothed.

The ashram concept is now a part of a movement worldwide in scope. Part-time ashrams have spread across the United States, Europe, and Japan. Group movements, with varying emphases and outlooks, are attempts to put the **koinonia** back into the church. They have their dangers, one of them being that they sometimes produce another sect with a holier-than-thou attitude. The Ashram movement is not immune to that danger. But we are alive to it. We do not believe that the Ashram movement is the Way. All we can say is that it is a way to the Way. Jesus is the Way. We try to come out at his feet.

In a word an ashram is not just a place; it is a total experience in corporate, disciplined Christian living. The program balances devotional practice, study, corporate worship, and manual work in a totality of committed life together. It is an experiment and experience in family living in which we even address each other as Sister Mary or Brother Stanley. It aims at being an experience of the Kingdom of God—in miniature. It presupposes a heart open to God, and it is an experience in which the sincere seekers end up with a heart over-flowing with love of God and neighbor. No wonder it has caught on wherever in the world it has been tried—for it meets a universal need with a universal Christ.—September, 1972, Sat Tal

———◆———

Eternal life is not merely a description of duration, but it is a description of the quality of life. That is important. A man said to me, "I do not believe in the future life, because I would not like to live with myself forever." So Jesus talks about the quality of life, as well as duration of life eternal. You are living a quality of life that makes it possible for you to love yourself because self is a lovable term. I like myself because Jesus is changing me into my becoming. The self comes into new birth. It is a kind of self which is fit for survival.—September, 1972, Sat Tal

———◆———

If I say to a group of people, "What do you believe?" they will go apart, no two believing exactly alike. But if I say, "Whom do you trust?" they come together with one word on their lips—Jesus Christ. The "whats" divide but the "whom" unites by his very nature. So the Divine Yes is not a system or a party for an organization of any kind. It is a relationship with a Person, a universal Person who is universally relevant. For Jesus is the same yesterday, today, and forever. He has always been relevant; he is relevant today and will be forever relevant. Heaven is heaven because he is there to be universally loved and obeyed. Hell is where there is general disorder for there is no relevancy in any one person or group outside of Jesus. So when the search for relevancy and the emphasis is on Jesus, it holds together the past, present, and future. It isn't outdated or outmoded, for Jesus isn't. Wherever

Jesus is, there is Home. Therefore he is relevant always.—October, 1972, Sat Tal

———◆———

The happiest person I have ever seen in my life was a dying woman. As she was dying she clapped her hands in joy. She even joked, "I am literally being tickled to death." Many were converted by her bedside, including her own son. When the people had gone, I knelt beside her bed. I could not pray for her. She had everything, including death in her possession. But she could pray for me. She kept her hand on my head and prayed that I might preach the Gospel of Joy in the face of life and death. Now I have been ordained. But the mightiest ordination I have ever had was not by a bishop, but by a dying woman. When I stand up to preach, I can feel her hand upon my head, ordaining me to preach the Gospel of Joy in spite of life and death.—October, 1972, Sat Tal

———◆———

Lately I have been thinking about the Gospel passage, Matthew 17:1-9. This incident of Moses and Elijah, speaking to Jesus on the Mount of Transfiguration, has very pointed reference to leading from the outer world. Can the dead guide the living? Here was a case in point. Moses and Elijah reporting from another world said that he (Jesus) must go through with his departure at Jerusalem, that self-giving love, sacrificial love, is the central fact of the Christian faith. He must go through with it. Can the dead govern, guide, and control the living? When Peter tried to make permanent this attitude of the other world controlling this one by erecting three tabernacles, a cloud came over them and a voice came from the cloud: "This is my beloved Son, **hear him**" (Mark 9:7). So don't be expecting the dead to guide you. You are to be guided by the Son of Man, the Son of God. This puts the other world in its place. You are not to depend upon the other world for guidance in this one. That would be man, once alive, now so-called dead, guiding people who are now living. We have but one Master and Lord, Jesus Christ.—October, 1972, Sat Tal

The United Methodist Baltimore Conference Historical Society has offered me a grave plot in the Bishops' Lot in Mt. Olivet Cemetery on Frederick Road in Baltimore. Here Francis Asbury and other bishops are buried. The cemetery is about one hundred yards from where I got into the Kingdom of God, for the former site of the Memorial Methodist Church, the place of my conversion, was next to the cemetery. So when they asked me if I could be buried there, I said, "Well, it is within a hundred yards of where I got into the Kingdom of God, and it would be a homecoming." So I consented.

Incidentally, my son-in-law, Bishop Mathews, said jokingly to me, "This isn't fair. You don't have the troubles of the bishops, but you get buried with them!" My reply was, "I may not have the troubles of the bishops, in their administrative and pastoral care for the churches, but I was a bishop for twenty-four hours and then resigned in Kansas City, Missouri, at the General Conference there in 1928. My joy came back when I resigned, for I was called by God to be an evangelist and a missionary.—November, 1972, Sat Tal

———◆———

Never have I emphasized "being in heaven" very much in my life, for I think I have had heaven here. Heaven is first a condition, then a place. Finding Jesus as Savior and Lord and the Kingdom of God as the ultimate goal of the world and humanity has been sufficient to keep my faith in a world called heaven. So heaven is a state of mind and heart and a quality of being, before it is a place. I do not see how I could accept the place without the state of being, for if there is no heaven where do I grow up? I know better how to live now at eighty-eight than I did at eighteen or twenty-eight, even though I am still an uncompleted person. Nonetheless, heaven is in that state of mind and heart primarily within. If at the end when I get out there and find there is no heaven, I will say, "Well, universe, you let me down. You had the feeling of the eternal and the real, but I see there is no heaven, nothing but a cipher, emptiness. But I am not sorry I was a Christian. Give me back my choices to make over and I would say, 'Heaven or no heaven, I'm a Christian by conviction and choice.' It doesn't take heaven to make me glad of that."—November, 1972, Sat Tal

———◆———

Now that I am in this crisis I face the question of living on crippled or calling it a day and accepting a

147

passage to the other world. I am honestly indifferent as to which it shall be. I don't know what the future holds, but I know who holds it. I have tried for eighty-eight years (and in a few days it will be eighty-nine), and I have no need to live any more unless he decides. I have often said half jokingly that when I get to heaven, I will ask for twenty-four hours to see my friends, and then I shall go up to him and say, "Haven't you a world somewhere which has fallen people who need an evangelist like me? Please send me there." For I know no heaven beyond preaching the Gospel to people. That is heaven to me. It has been, is, and ever shall be heaven to me.—December, 1972, Sat Tal

It says in the New English Bible in John 11:25, "I am the resurrection and I am life," leaving out the second "the" before life. Then Jesus is not only resurrection in his own resurrection, but in the lives of those whom he resurrected. Life took on new freshness because he is Resurrection and Life. Wherever he comes, there is resurrection. He is the principle and power of resurrection. Resurrection when Jesus comes is not just physical, but mental, spiritual, social, economic, and every other way. He is Resurrection and Life. No one can come in contact with him without resurrection.—December, 1972, Sat Tal

Sometimes I find myself musing in this way: Dear old body—for the past nine decades we've walked the dusty roads together, we've flown across continents, and you've been uncomplaining even when I've put impossible loads upon you. Thank you for your faithful service, and now you say you'll be faithful till death us do part. When that parting comes, I'll look back at you and salute you and thank you, and I'll say to you, "When I get my immortal body, I hope there will be a lot of you there incorporated." Thank you again, for everything.—**January, 1973, Sat Tal**

Returning again to John 11:25, the New English Bible translation says, "I am the resurrection and I am life." If "the" can be left out before **life** I do not see why it cannot be left out before resurrection: I am resurrection and life. If it would mean anything, it would mean: I am an instance of resurrection, but I am also the principle and power of resurrection. The Bible says one who has constant contact with resurrection will never die. If he may die in one part of him, he may become more powerful in other parts. Physically he may die in a worn-out body, but he will be renewed in spirit.

I have often said that when the people stand around and say, "Well, Brother Stanley is gone," I want to be able to wink at them, and if I have enough strength, I would like to laugh and say, "Jesus is Lord." Because this will not be death. It will be fuller life. I say this as a half joke, but I believe it will turn out to be reality. Because any person who is in Jesus is deathless, for he is under the principle and power of resurrection.—**January, 1973, Sat Tal**

———————◆———————

PRAYER: Dear God, put thy hand upon us as we go forth knowing that the Divine Yes is at last sounded and is the Yes that affirms all the promises of God. They come to their fruition in him. The world is going to find it out—and what a turning and what an opportunity and what an open door it will be. In Jesus' name we ask it. Amen.

POSTSCRIPT

On the morning of January 25, 1973, Dr. E. Stanley
Jones breathed his last. His death took place in Clara
that he should have died there, amidst a land and a
general hospital, Clara Swain Hospital significantly,
was founded as the first hospital for women in all of
Asia. Moreover, Bareilly was where Methodism was
launched in India in 1856. It was somehow appropriate
that he should have died there, amidst a land and a
people he dearly loved. He was surrounded by a few
friends and devoted doctors and nurses of the hospital.
Death came to him peacefully.

It was his desire, often repeated and given to us in
his own handwriting, that should he die in India his
remains should be cremated. This was done and a por-
tion of his ashes have been interred in the Bishops' Lot

of Mt. Olivet Cemetery, Baltimore. The remainder are buried at the Ashram in his beloved Sat Tal in the Himalayas at the very spot he had pointed out to us on various occasions, a lovely knoll called Phyllis Mount.

Many people have asked about his last months. As this book has stated he was stricken by a paralytic stroke on the night of December 7, 1971. It was a brainstem stroke which immobilized his left arm and leg as well as the right side of his face. His eyesight was also affected. The voice that had thrilled thousands with Christ's Gospel was almost stilled, reduced to indistinct mumblings. In all he had preached sixty thousand sermons—probably more than any other man in history. Though his mind remained clear, the passion of his life—to make Jesus Christ known and loved by all—was for the while at least brought to an end.

After two weeks in the Baptist Memorial Hospital in Oklahoma City, he was moved to Boston to be near his daughter and family. He was treated at several hospitals in that city. These hospitals were to be his home for the next five months. During that period he marked his eighty-eighth birthday. He liked to joke and stated on that occasion: "Life is fun at eighty-eight—and getting funnier all the time!"

By the middle of May, 1972, he had become quite restless. Though there had been some improvement in his physical condition, he felt a kind of medical prisoner. As he himself reports, the doctors were understanding and saw no reason for his being confined. They readily consented to his fervent desire once more to return to India.

The account of that trip is a story unto itself. I had

the privilege of escorting him, accompanied by his granddaughter, an occupational therapist, and his teen-age grandson and namesake who acted as "muscle man." Suffice it to say that we arrived safely in India, to be greeted by blast-furnace heat of 117 degrees! Twenty-four hours later we arrived at beautiful Sat Tal and the Ashram there.

The specialists in Boston said he would never walk again and never preach again. I can remember vividly how he asked me: "Jim, will you help me walk again?" Almost without realizing what I was saying, I replied, "Yes."

At first our efforts at Sat Tal were dismal failures, and I concluded that the doctors in Boston knew what they were talking about. Then we prayed—prayed around the clock, twenty-four hours a day—for a week. We fasted and prayed. In addition we used such common sense as we possessed. We built a kind of wooden "track" which prevented his stumbling as it guided his paralyzed foot. We blindfolded one eye, for at first he dimly saw the "track" double. We used a four-legged cane for his "good" right arm. We employed massage, for every Indian seems to have a natural gift as masseur or masseuse. Sainted octogenarian, Sister Lulu, was particularly helpful in this ministry. We helped develop a rhythm for the right sequence of movement of feet and cane. At first we counted the cadence for him, but the next day he said, "Don't count. I'm counting to myself."

But most of all we found all over again that walking is always a matter of faith. Again and again we read to him the story of the lame man healed at the beautiful gate of the Temple in Jerusalem (Acts 3). To begin our walking lessons we would say to him: "In the name of Jesus Christ of Nazareth, walk" (Acts 3:6). And he did—at first falteringly, and then a few steps with fuller assurance. At first we supported him. Then I reminded him of the words he had addressed to his daughter and me when we were married: "I never want to be in the way—nor out of the way if you need me." I spoke the same words back to him. It was "hands off" unless he began to fall.

In a word, after a week, this man who was never supposed to walk again was walking as far as fifty feet. Finally, he could walk as far as half a mile and climb up and down steps too. Moreover, this man, who after sixty thousand sermons was never supposed to preach again, did preach six times in my hearing within a week. Altogether during his final year he preached about fifty times. I last saw him at the end of November, 1972. He completed this book on his eighty-ninth birthday, January 3, 1973. When I last saw him he was walking, walking with God, and—like Enoch of old—God took him!

His death came only two weeks before he intended to return with his nephew, Everett Jones, to consult an ophthalmologist in Atlanta, a physician in whom he had great confidence. After that he wished to return once more to India. For he was always by faith looking ahead. This trip was not to be.

What are we to say of such a life? The tributes to him have been many and have come from all over the world. Here are a few:

The sympathy which we would extend to you at the news of your father's going somehow seems to be caught up into a grand doxology in which many on both sides of the great divide give thanks and praise to God for a marvellous song of ascents, which came to a climax in a grand finale of victorious living—because Jesus is Lord! So be it!

The final victory has come for him who taught so many thousands the secret of victorious living. The world can never be the same again because he passed this way.

Seldom in Church history have so many owed so much to one Prophet of God.

To speak of Dr. E. Stanley Jones is to acknowledge him as missionary of Christ, as evangelist, as Christian statesman, and as advocate and citizen of the Kingdom of God. Not often does a son-in-law have occasion to tell his father-in-law where to go. In 1970, however, it was my privilege to preside over the final session of the North India Conference of which Stanley Jones had been long a member. Anyone privy to the mysteries of Methodism knows that at the end of a conference the bishop reads out the appointments of the preachers. When I came to his name, I appointed him "ambassador extraordinary and minister plenipotentiary of the Kingdom of God!"

The last time I conversed with him at the Clara Swain Hospital, we laughed together and prayed together. By chance I had just met Madame Vijayalaksmi Pandit in New Delhi. She is a sister of Jawaharlal Nehru and aunt of Prime Minister of Indira Gandhi. I asked her if she wanted to send regards to Dr. Jones. She replied, "No, not my regards; my love. Our whole family has always held him in the highest respect." He was delighted with this word. We conversed about his work. The emphasis was more on the future than on the past.

For thirty-five years I knew him intimately and had occasion to observe him closely for prolonged periods. He rang true! Of course, he had weaknesses. These were before the Lord, for he was completely surrendered to Jesus Christ. Once, when I asked a Hindu how he was, he replied, "As you see me." So it was with Brother Stanley, as he was called. He was as you saw him.

Oh, how he loved India! He knew the land and its people intimately for he had traveled for more than half a century into every corner of the country and had become acquainted with high and low alike. When first he went to India in 1907, he said that one word stood for India: paralysis! When he came toward the end of his years there, he said the word was **possibility!**

Brother Stanley was a highly disciplined person. When he was in college, he developed the practice of two hours of prayer and meditation daily. And he continued in this habit. Morning and evening he would simply slip away for his hours of devotion. Because of this, he was the despair of hostesses who wanted their guests to enjoy the marvelous conversation of which he was capable.

His discipline included filling his every waking hour with reading, writing, counseling, and speaking. Each day, too, was closed with some type of rigorous physical exercise. He continued to be a fine baseball and tennis player.

Moreover, he was a superb preacher. At his best many regard him as the most effective interpreter of the Gospel in contemporary terms that they ever heard. They marvel when they contrast his preaching with what all too often passes for evangelism in our day. For him there was no contradiction between being the Old Testament prophet and the New Testament evangelist. The two belong together, as response to the Gospel and obedience to the Gospel belong together!

John Wesley once said that Christians should "gain all they can, save all they can, and give all they can." The early Methodists responded to the first two admonitions, but often balked on the third. E. Stanley Jones practiced all three. We can testify that he quite literally gave away all he had—the nearly one million dollars that he earned as royalties on his books. As a result thousands of young people were provided with the means of higher education.

In a great many ways Stanley Jones was a pioneer—a man before his time.

He spoke out for racial justice even in the Deep South at a time when it was not popular to do so. He insisted that his meetings be open to all peoples regardless of race.

He stood for peace when that, too, was not a favored cause. Until the very last moment he was found busy trying to prevent war between the United States and Japan. He was several times nominated for the Nobel Peace Prize.

With respect to the matter of church union, he advocated this with integrity to all traditions. The people heard him gladly and with acceptance on this thorny subject. I have never been convinced that something very like his notion of federal union might not yet result in serious and effective union among the churches of the United States.

Today the virtues of corporate life are often extolled. He lived much of the time for years in an Ashram—a kind of disciplined religious commune. For him the Kingdom of God was to be taken seriously.

He was a global person in the most specific sense—long before globality became a general reality. He had been simply everywhere. A missionary first of all to India, E. Stanley Jones became a missionary to the whole world. For fifty years he lived quite literally out of a suitcase.

Today the holistic understanding and approach are much favored. Tertullian could say that the soul was naturally Christian. Stanley Jones extended this: the whole body was naturally Christian—nerves, blood vessels, vital organs, the mind—the whole of society was meant for Christian love.

For some people dialogue between the Christian faith and other secular and religious faiths is a new thing. For years in his Round Table conferences he was engaged in this approach with adherents of every religious persuasion and every ideology throughout Asia. Indeed, he can be said to have had more concrete experience of this than any other person has ever had.

For those who would like to be confronted more freely with this remarkable career of total Christian witness, I refer to his autobiography, **A Song of**

Ascents. It was my privilege to write an introduction to that volume. I take liberty to repeat here my assessment of his achievements:

———◆———

He found the Christian movement largely among the outcastes and left it at the center of India's life, a challenge and an issue to the intellectuals and leaders.

He found the Christian movement scattering its energies about marginal issues of doctrine and denominations and left it centered on Jesus Christ as the one and central issue.

He found the Christian movement largely alien and Western and left it more naturalized through the Ashram movement.

He found the Ashram movement Indian and localized and left it internationalized and universalized.

He found evangelism in America on the edges of the life of the churches, largely in marginal groups, and not too respectable and in good odor; and he left it a central issue in the life of all the churches and made it respectable and necessary.

He found evangelism largely emotional and left it appealing to the total person—mind, spirit, and body.

He found Christianity presented as alien to human nature and left it as supernaturally natural and sin as unnatural and alien.

He found the Kingdom of God largely inward and mystical, or futuristic in heaven, and put it into life as the one issue now, supplanting all the alternatives of communism, fascism, and whatnot. The Kingdom of God on earth and on earth now is the issue.

The Divine Yes

He found the nonviolent noncooperation movement Indian and Gandhian and left it as a method of finding freedom for the Negroes of America.

He found church union alternating between church councils and merger and put in between them federal union as a practical plan for union now.

———————◆———————

Thanks be unto God for E. Stanley Jones. Jesus is Lord!

James K. Mathews
Washington, D.C.